HEIDEGGER AND THE PROBLEM OF CONSCIOUSNESS

HEIDEGGER AND THE PROBLEM OF CONSCIOUSNESS

Nancy J. Holland

Indiana University Press

This book is a publication of

Indiana University Press
Office of Scholarly Publishing
Herman B Wells Library 350
1320 East 10th Street
Bloomington, Indiana 47405 USA

iupress.indiana.edu

Manufactured in the United States of America

Library of Congress Cataloging-in-Publication Data

Names: Holland, Nancy J. (Nancy Jean), author.
Title: Heidegger and the problem of consciousness / Nancy J. Holland, Indiana
    University Press.
Description: Bloomington : Indiana University Press, 2018. | Includes
    bibliographical references and index.
Identifiers: LCCN 2018015671 (print) | LCCN 2018020404 (ebook) | ISBN
    9780253035967 (ebook) | ISBN 9780253035950 (alk. paper) | ISBN
    9780253035943 (alk. paper)
Subjects: LCSH: Heidegger, Martin, 1889-1976. | Consciousness. | Mind and
    body.
Classification: LCC B3279.H49 (ebook) | LCC B3279.H49 H56 2018 (print) | DDC
    128/.2092—dc23
LC record available at https://lccn.loc.gov/2018015671

1 2 3 4 5   23 22 21 20 19 18

This book is dedicated to the memory of my teachers:
John Mothershead
Phillip H. Rhinelander
Paul Feyerabend
Hubert L. Dreyfus

Contents

Acknowledgments

I WOULD LIKE to thank Marjolein Oele and Gerard Kuperus, the editors of *Ontologies of Nature: Continental Perspectives and Environmental Reorientations*, for providing me with the initial opportunity to develop the basic argument of this book and for their invaluable help in making it clearer and more accurate. Dee Mortensen and three anonymous reviewers for Indiana University Press also made significant contributions to my thinking, especially with regard to the secondary literature. I would also like to acknowledge the special efforts of the staff at Indiana University Press in the final stages of the preparation of the manuscript for publication.

Hamline University supported the writing of this book through a sabbatical leave; my study of the work of Gerald Edelman through a Hanna Faculty Development Grant; and my first reading of *The Essence of Truth* through a Summer Collaborative Research Grant. Hamline Faculty Development grants also supported my travel to the meetings of the Society for Phenomenology and Existential Philosophy where I heard Elisabeth Grosz and Geoffrey Bennington speak.

Finally, many thanks to my Hamline colleague Gary Gabor for help with, and fascinating conversations about, Aristotle's (and Heidegger's) Greek.

HEIDEGGER AND THE PROBLEM OF CONSCIOUSNESS

Charlemagne's Monogram

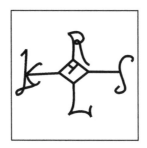

And yet is any problem more novel today than that of consciousness?
—Jacques Derrida (*Psyché: Inventions of the Other, Volume II*, 2008)

Consider the above monogram of Charles the Great, also known as Charlemagne. It is read starting from the K at the left, through the small A at the upper corner of the internal square, to the R, back through the O formed by the square, to the lower L, up through the U formed by the bottom of the square (clearer in reproductions where the path is highlighted in gold), and ending with the S at the far right—Karolus (Latin for Charles). There is an inside to the monogram and an outside, but they are inextricably linked, both physically in the monogram and in use.[1] What is outside (the consonants) has meaning only in the context of the active movement that generates or forms the emptiness inside (the vowels). Without movement, neither vowels, consonants, nor meaning exist at all. (The gold sometimes used to mark the path of the vowels underscores, most likely by accident, the primary role of movement in the monogram's functioning.)

This image, found everywhere in Aachen, Charlemagne's capital, can serve as an icon for the Heideggerian understanding of consciousness. The center is empty, a nullity, as he says in *Being and Time* (e.g., Heidegger 1962, 354), but it is not unmarked or featureless. It is marked both by its very emptiness (the O and the U) and by the uniqueness of its own situation (the A). From this center, Dasein moves out, not randomly, but in the ways determined by the world in which it finds itself (in this case, language) to give meaning to its existence. And it always brings that world back into itself in meaning-giving activity. "This means that, for its part, the material as such refers beyond itself," both to its basis in what is outside us and to the meaningful world in which we encounter it (Heidegger 2008, 43). The world Dasein encounters—for example, the early Medieval European world that bowed to a Holy Roman Emperor unable to write his own name—is not of its own making, but given to it to live as its own. Likewise, the meanings it generates are never its own but always social, not in the sense of a collectivity, but in the sense in which a language and a history are social and shared. The natural world, "the physical," is a manifestation of, and exists as such only for, consciousness, "the mental". Without Dasein, stuff would move around, things would happen, living beings would emerge, live, and die, but there would be no facts, no laws, no beings as the beings that they are.

Heidegger seems to suggest something similar in "On the Question of Being" when, after striking out the word "being" with a large X, he states, "the sign of this crossing through cannot, however, be the merely negative sign of a crossing out. It points, rather, toward the four regions of the fourfold and their being gathered in the locale of this crossing through." He appears to mean that each end of the two lines used to strike out the word "being" can be seen as an arrow pointing outward from the now "empty" place of the word toward the fourfold of earth, sky, gods, and mortals—and as arrows in the reverse direction that meet at the center of the nullified "being" to draw these four elements together to create our existence. From this link between human existence and the negation, or crossing out, of being, he draws the conclusion that "the human essence, in its thoughtful commemoration, belongs to the nothing, and not merely as some addition" (Heidegger 1998, 310–11). In both cases—the monogram and the crossing out of "being"—the ec-static movement away from the nothing that we are and toward that which gives us our world is the hallmark of our existence as Dasein.

Note

1. I use the terms "inside" and "outside" with more than a little trepidation for lack of better ones. Heidegger himself warns us, "life [like the monogram] is so constituted as to lack an 'outside' and an 'inside' in an Objectively objective sense" (Heidegger 2001, 88).

1 Introduction

> One can, in fact, discuss exclusively the fundamental issues, but what is discussed does not have to include everything.
>
> —Martin Heidegger (*Logic: The Question of Truth*, 2010)

I: Heidegger, Nature, and Consciousness

A recent article in the *Journal of the American Philosophical Association* asks, "Is Consciousness a Spandrel?" In other words, did phenomenal consciousness (i.e., our lived experience of the world) evolve along with the complexity of the human brain, but without contributing to (or inhibiting) the evolutionary success of the species, so that everything would be exactly as it is if we had no phenomenal consciousness at all? The authors argue that, yes, phenomenal consciousness is a "by-product" of evolution, much like blood type or eye color.[1]

The reasons for adopting such a position are clear. Phenomenal consciousness is inherently and necessarily subjective and, hence, beyond the reach of objective, scientific investigation. Furthermore, if the material world is a closed causal system, phenomenal consciousness must be either physical to act causally in that system, or, as the article argues, evolutionarily useless. This should be considered closely for a moment. To say that consciousness is a spandrel means that beings much like ourselves, but lacking phenomenal consciousness, could build a world in which they could not see the color of a leaf, yet still discovered chlorophyll; could not hear music as music, yet produced Beethoven's Fifth Symphony; could not be aware of the stars, yet sent a spacecraft past Pluto; could not understand puzzles, yet produced Sherlock Holmes; and could have no experience of pain or grief, yet developed modern medicine and philosophy.

I will not try to refute the authors' argument. Given their assumptions, it might well be irrefutable. It is those assumptions that interest me. They illuminate the fact that, after four hundred years, philosophy may have immensely refined the mind/body dichotomy that plays a central role in the thought of René Descartes, but it has not managed to resolve the paradoxes it generates. Rather than argue in those terms, this book will follow the lead of Descartes's contemporary Baruch Spinoza. He responded to Descartes's dualism not by redefining the mental in a way that would make it compatible with our understanding of the physical—as most contemporary philosophers attempt to do—but by redefining the physical in a way that would make it compatible with our lived experience as conscious beings.

I was spurred to embark on this task by a claim Martin Heidegger makes as part of his implicit critique of science (or scientism) in the 1932 lectures collected in *The Essence of Truth*. There, he states that the connections between things with which science concerns itself in the physical world "are *there* only in so far as they are reckoned with—how so? By perceiving and experiencing and dealing (and so forth) with beings" (Heidegger 2002a, 161). I argue that this is not a reformulation of George Berkeley's "*esse percipi*," but rather a reminder that science exists only as a human activity undertaken for human purposes. That is, the objects of science exist as things of a particular kind only in the context of specific scientific enterprises and research programs. In our current state of knowledge, to take a well-known example, light can be conceptualized as a particle or a wave without actually being either, but the physics of light progresses all the same. The things about which and with which science reckons exist in our scientific world in the first place because, and insofar as, they are reckoned with.

It is important to note that what I have to say about Heidegger here would leave the sciences free to be what they are, though they would be repositioned as partial, secondary, and primarily instrumental forms of understanding rather than the measure of all knowledge they have become since Descartes. In Heidegger's view, as we will see, there are multiple layers of truth in any social context. Some of these layers are obvious and easily accessed (e.g., "ordinary science"), and some are more obscure and possibly less rationally based, as Thomas Kuhn has argued. There are also deeper layers that resist any easy analysis. These include the complex interwoven belief systems represented in the thirteenth-to-fifteenth century mosaic ceiling of the Baptistery in Florence, as well as the convention that applies the word "clan" to premodern and early modern Scotland, but not the word "tribe." Still deeper we hit a kind of bedrock—not an eternal truth, but one very slow to change. As Ludwig Wittgenstein says, our "spade is turned" (Wittgenstein 2009, 91).

Heidegger's concern, however, is only secondarily with the way modern science and technology distort our relationship with beings (i.e., the natural world seen as nothing more than a collection of calculable masses in motion). His primary concern is with how science and technology distort our understanding of ourselves (i.e., as "minds" in relation to, and potentially explainable in terms of, a subset of the calculable masses we call "human bodies"). My claim is that if we begin from the merely physical, we can never explain how or why consciousness exists. We are left with the spandrel argument or something similar. Only by rethinking the physical from the starting point of our lived experience can we ever hope to solve the problem established by Descartes's dualistic conjecture. The rethinking of our relationship to the natural world that I see in Heidegger's work is based on Dasein's constant "reckoning with," or directedness toward, beings, as well as the insight that things can exist for us only as experienced. This idea is, of course, Kantian in origin, but Kant's account of the "phenomenal" remains far too abstract. Put somewhat differently, our knowledge of the world is built not from the outside in through perception, but from the inside out—from the tacit knowing inherent in our day-to-day involvement with things toward what has become contemporary technology/science.[2]

That said, it is easier to explain what this present study *is not* rather than what it is. It is not an exhaustive study of Heidegger's work, nor does it offer a comprehensive interpretation of his thought. It is not an attempt to determine his proper place in the pantheon of twentieth-century German or European philosophy. It is not a defense of, or apology for, his involvement with the Nazi party, nor for the undeniable sexism, racism, heterosexism, anti-Semitism, and other biases that can be found in his words. I am not particularly interested in whether there is a clear demarcation between Heidegger's thought and, for example, Husserl's (though I am among the many who believe there is), Rather, I am primarily interested in whether Heidegger's understanding of human consciousness opens up new avenues for philosophical problem-solving more effectively than does Husserl.[3]

I view this work as part of a new wave of twenty-first-century Heidegger scholarship that moves beyond these preoccupations to seek in Heidegger's texts the tools with which philosophy might better address not only the mind/body problem, but also the mounting ecological crisis and other issues that must be addressed in ways that do not relegate human consciousness to spandrel status. Jacques Derrida calls this a "neo-Heideggerian" way of thinking (Derrida 2005, 216). In his foreword to the English translation of Michel Haar's *Heidegger and the Essence of Man*, Hubert Dreyfus suggests that we need to find a middle path between a "long line of Germanic treatises that have reverently repeated Heidegger's jargon and numerous French-style essays that have irreverently attempted to deconstruct Heidegger and go beyond him" (Haar 1993, xv).[4] The present book, like much other recent work on Heidegger, is such an attempt to find such a middle path.[5]

My examination moves from *Towards the Definition of Philosophy* (1919) to *Four Seminars* (1966–73) in an exploration of the groundwork Heidegger laid for a radical rethinking of how we understand our relationship to the physical and social worlds. I argue that his concern with the relationship between consciousness and the physical began very early in his thinking, and that this element of his thought has been systematically misunderstood or distorted. The misunderstanding arises because of the very phenomenon he identifies—the tendency to see ourselves as subjects in relation to objects on the Cartesian/Husserlian model of intentionality.[6] By tracing his line of thought from the "early Heidegger" to the later work on Greek philosophy and technology and by de-emphasizing *Being and Time*, the present book will also suggest a new approach to the so-called *Kehre* and present a unified interpretation of Heidegger's work across the span of his philosophical career.[7]

The remainder of this introductory chapter will clarify the difference between "nature" and φύσις for Heidegger and explain how that difference links his understanding of "nature" with the fundamental relationship of "Western historical man" to himself. It also offers a parallel consideration of the relationship between ψυχή and modern concepts of consciousness and the mental. In the second chapter, I will describe current interpretations of the problem of consciousness as they appear in the neurobiological work of Gerald Edelman, in some areas of philosophical psychology and cognitive science, and in psychologist Max Velmans's *Understanding Consciousness*.

In the subsequent five chapters, I will trace Heidegger's understanding of and approach to this problem throughout his career. The third chapter focuses on the very early lectures, where this line of thought first appears. The fourth chapter traces the same themes through the period leading up to and including *Being and Time*. The fifth chapter looks at some key text of the *Kehre*, which many scholars regard as a major turning point in Heidegger's thought, with special emphasis on "On the Essence of Truth." The sixth chapter carries the argument forward through *The Essence of Truth* and "The Origin of the Work of Art." The seventh chapter follows these themes along the two paths Heidegger takes in his work after 1940—ancient Greek philosophy and the critique of modern technology—with a coda from his lectures of the 1960s and 1970s. The final chapter addresses how my interpretation of Heidegger articulates with, challenges, and is challenged by the work of prominent "third-generation" readings of Heidegger, including those of Hubert Dreyfus, Richard Capobianco, Thomas Sheehan, and Jacques Derrida. Unlike Sheehan, I will not pretend to "make sense" of Heidegger. My primary purpose is to shed a clearer light on the groundwork Heidegger lays for a radical, and necessary, rethinking of both nature and our lived experience. This rethinking will allow us to see that relationship beyond the limits of the mind/body dichotomy.

II: Nature as (Not) Φύσις

Although I use the terms "nature" and "the physical" more or less interchangeably, this equivalence was not strictly allowed for by Heidegger himself.[8,9] The key for understanding Heidegger's rejection of the Latin translation of φύσις as "nature" can be found in his lectures on Aristotle's *Physics*, but important stages of the argument can also be found in other lecture courses from the mid-1930s. In *Introduction to Metaphysics* (1935), for example, he notes, "We use the Latin translation *natura*, which really means 'to be born', 'birth.' But with this Latin translation, the original content of the Greek word *phusis* is already thrust aside, the authentic philosophical naming force of the Greek word is destroyed." According to Heidegger, for the Greeks, "*Phusis* is Being itself" (Heidegger 2000, 14–15).[10]

Heidegger's interpretation of the meaning of φύσις in Aristotle's text might be clearer if we remember that the ancient Greek world recognized little that would fall into the category of completely "dead" matter as we understand it today. Stones, mud, and dirt might qualify (cf. Plato's "Parmenides"), but even they are not totally inert. Not every kind of clay (a sort of mud) can be used for all purposes. Similarly, marble has an internal structure that prevents it from being sculpted into certain shapes. The metals available in ancient times also placed many constraints on how they could be used for human purposes compared with the steel and aluminum we use today. Iron rusts and shatters; gold and copper are relatively soft. There is, thus, a continuum between these inorganic materials and such organic materials as wood, ivory, and leather. This continuum blurs the sharp modern distinction between the mineral and the vegetable or animal. The ancients lived in a world that was alive through and through—not because they were ignorant or superstitious, but because they seldom encountered anything that did not have an intrinsic structure that limited their use of it.

We can begin to unpack Heidegger's claim that "*Phusis* is Being itself" by looking at his lectures in the *Physics*. There, he cites Aristotle's claim that it is "ridiculous to attempt to prove *that* φύσις is," and he translates the explanation that follows by noting that "wherever a being from φύσις stands in the open, φύσις has already shown itself and stands in view" (Heidegger 1999, 240). A "being from φύσις" refers not to the difference between the organic and the inorganic, as it would in the modern world, but to the distinction between things that appear "naturally" as opposed to things that are human-made. Human artifacts imply the existence of humans; "natural" objects imply the existence of nature. For Aristotle, according to Heidegger, "we find what is φύσις-like only where there is μορφή"—usually translated as "form." Form serves a dual role here; it takes the place of human intent in giving shape to natural objects, and it links the objects to their final cause, replacing human purpose. "Thus μορφή constitutes the Being of φύσις, or at least *co*-constitutes it" (Heidegger 1999, 251; his emphasis, my interpolation).

Heidegger further notes that in nature, "each being that is *pro*-duced or put *forth* (excluding artifacts) is also put *away*, as the blossom is put away by the fruit. But in this putting *away*, the placing into appearance—φύσις—does not cease to be" (Heidegger 1999, 267; his emphasis). Nature is a plentitude; it never *is* and then *is not*. It "abhors a vacuum," as the more recent formulation puts it. For Aristotle, there is no sharp break. One form or phase of a natural process does not replace another so that it is now this, now not this but that. Rather, the matter (ὕλη) of the entity transforms into the next phase, while the previous phase lingers as that from which the later phase developed ("morphed" [middle voice] as we now say). For example, the remnants of the blossom remain at the bottom of the fruit, and diamonds retain the crystalline structure of the carbon atoms in the graphite from which the gemstones were made.

This is the point at which the origin of "nature," in reference to the Latin concept of birth, comes into question. Although birth is an organic process, it is also a rupture with the source, rather than a continuation of the source. The result is an individual distinct from the mother that can continue to exist even in her absence. The verb form of the Greek φύσις, φύειν, means to grow, to engender, or to bring forth. These expressions suggest agricultural analogies more than maternal ones. Birth is a special case of natural change—one in which most of the transformative process is hidden—so the result appears suddenly as a *fait accompli*. Nature, as understood in terms of maternal production of a new entity, is more compatible than φύσις with the modern view of natural processes as a "change of material" in which inert matter is reorganized by external forces to form something new, while the previous form ceases to exist.[11]

Thus, any text examining Heidegger's work must always use the word "nature" with implicit scare quotes. Even "physical" has limitations as a substitute, because it evokes modern physics or, worse, modern concepts of the material world as it is understood in the hierarchical opposition between mind and matter. No other word, in English or in German is appropriate, and φύσις is not appropriate because it is not ours. That ancient Greek word has its true meaning, based on its materiality and sound, only in a world to which we do not belong and cannot fully understand.

III: Ψυχή/Mind/Consciousness

Much the same can be said of ψυχή. As previously noted, Heidegger sometimes uses this Greek word rather than "mental" or "conscious(ness)" for the same reason that he prefers φύσις to "nature." He believes that the Latin *mens* and *conscius*, and hence the English terms derived from them, distort and pervert the meaning of the original Greek. Nevertheless, I generally use the usual English words, because I find them to be justifiable substitutions, given that Aristotle's book on ψυχή covers many of the topics familiar from the contemporary philosophy of mind. By contrast, many of the topics from his book on φύσις are no longer considered part of "physics."[12]

Still, it is important to understand how Heidegger views what he calls in his early work "the psychic." According to Heidegger, when Aristotle assimilates the relationship between mind (ψυχή) and body to the one between form and matter, he is not simply agreeing with Descartes's claim in the "Sixth Meditation" that "I am not only lodged in my body as a pilot in a vessel, but ... very closely united to it" (Descartes 1976, 192). Rather, for Aristotle, "the soul or life of animals (their primary being as animate) is conceptually, too, their primary being; that is, it is their form and what-it-means-to-be a body of that kind" (Aristotle 1990, 151, Zeta 10, 1035b). That is, the soul is what animates or actualizes the material body and makes it the kind of biological structure that it is.

This is what the phenomenological return to lived experience would suggest. My lived hunger, for example, is not an "intentional" state (since it is neither directed toward a specific object nor primarily mental). Nor is it some Cartesian message sent from my material body to my immaterial mind (since it can affect the workings of the mind itself), or a material empirical event that "causes" me to engage in eating behavior (since it does not always cause me to do so). Rather, it is an integrated reaction to changes in my blood sugar levels, the fullness of my stomach, the aroma of food, and the social clues in my environment, such as the time of day or the sight of others enjoying a meal (since all of these factors can be manipulated to increase or decrease the experience of hunger).[13]

This way of linking Aristotle's understanding of φύσις with his account of a human body "formed" by a mind or soul suggests one possible approach to the similar link between Heidegger's rethinking of the contemporary concept of nature in relation to the Greek concept and his attempt to rethink consciousness. The configuration that takes shape here is an understanding of embodied mind as our "primary being." We understand or "reckon with" things around us for pragmatic purposes; they are not primarily objects of abstract knowledge. My hunger engages behavior meant to assuage it; that behavior involves doors, stairs, coins, machines, and paper containers that hold chocolate and nuts to raise my blood sugar. This is, for Heidegger, the primary way in which I live my life. Everything else—including the science that describes my hunger and its cessation in terms of calories and so on, without reference to the oral/tactile and olfactory/gustatory experience of eating candy—is derivative. Moreover, as we know from the later Heidegger, the modern, scientific, technological understanding of our world as a "standing reserve" mathematically ordered for manipulation and exploitation is not so much a false interpretation of reality as a perverse interpretation dangerous to the future habitability of our planet. Even worse, it is a profound and damaging misinterpretation of what we ourselves are.[14]

Notes

1. Zack Robinson, Corey J. Maley, and Gualtiero Piccinini, "Is Consciousness a Spandrel?"

2. Of course, the implicit metaphor here is inadequate, if not misleading since, as noted in the Prologue, "inner" and "outer" are among the philosophical concepts Heidegger questions in the texts under consideration in this book.

3. Although my reading of Heidegger disagrees with theirs on other points, Richard Capobianco, Hubert Dreyfus, Frederick Olafson, and Thomas Sheehan all make this argument, as does Jacques Derrida, albeit in a less unqualified way.

4. I should note that I do not find Haar's own attempt to find such a path persuasive. He seems to want to re-establish a priority for "man" and the human in philosophical thought without a sufficient account of why Heidegger found those terms not only problematic but also dangerous.

5. I should also note that, as will become clear in chapter 8, I believe there is more to French readings of Heidegger than Dreyfus suggests in his Foreword to Haar's book, although how deeply he means what he says there is open to interpretation, given his own work on the relationship between Michel Foucault's work and Heidegger's.

6. Even Dreyfus at times seems to suggest that Heidegger's aim is not to undermine the concept of intentionality and the mind/body, subject/object distinction on which it relies, but to make them more consonant with our actual lived experience, to argue "that there was a *more basic form of intentionality* than that of a self-sufficient individual subject," although his claim is *de facto* limited to the Heidegger of *Being and Time* (Dreyfus 1991, 2–3, my emphasis).

7. Again, despite our other differences of opinion, Capobianco, Olafson, and Sheehan share this view about the continuity of Heidegger's work.

8. Both terms, as well as "the physical world," are also found in English translations of Heidegger's work and in the secondary literature.

9. While my entire argument in this book originally appears, in abbreviated form, as a chapter in *Ontologies of Nature: Continental Perspectives and Environmental Reorientations*, edited by Gerard Kuperus and Marjolein Oele, and benefitted greatly from comments of the editors and other readers for that volume, this section is especially richer and more accurate as a result of those editorial interventions.

10. I will also spell "*physis*" with a "y" or a "u" as it is found in the texts I cite (since there seems to be no clear consensus on the correct transliteration), but will use a "y" in my own text when I do not use the Greek.

11. Compare "Modern Science, Metaphysics, and Mathematics" (1936), where Heidegger credits Newton with redefining nature as "the mode of variety of the changing positions of bodies" (Heidegger 1993, 288).

12. Even more often than in the case of φύσις, the translations and the secondary literature also use the English terms.

13. This is, obviously, a much broader subject than can be fully examined here—my purpose is only to give a reading of Aristotle that provides a possible basis for how Heidegger might interpret the complex inter-relationships at issue here. See also the discussion of ψυχή in the "Theaetetus" in chapter 3.

14. On what sort of damage this misinterpretation might do, see my *Ontological Humility*. There, as here, it is important to note that the dualistic structure of Western thinking goes back far before Descartes, but it take on a new power and urgency with the rise of techno-science and the modern nation-state.

2 The Problem of Consciousness

But strictly speaking, we cannot say there was a time when there were no human beings. At every *time*, there were and are and will be human beings, because time temporalizes itself only as long as there are human beings.

—Martin Heidegger (*Introduction to Metaphysics*, 2000)

Consequently, the "physical reality" that we *perceive* is actually a peculiarly *human* world.

—Max Velmans (*Understanding Consciousness*)

I: The Neurobiology of Consciousness

I am focusing on the work of Nobel Laureate Gerald Edelman in this discussion of the current state of the study of consciousness from the perspective of brain science, because his work in neurobiology has unexpected affinities with my interpretation of Heidegger's thought. In his last book, *Second Nature*, Edelman argues against reductionist approaches to consciousness and for an understanding of brain function that takes full account of our embodiment. Indeed, he emphasizes the role of behavior in brain function: "The brain's maps and connections are altered not only by what you sense but by how you move" (Edelman 2006, 24). He also echoes Heidegger's question about the relationship between the mind as an object of scientific investigation and the mind as what investigates from his 1919 lectures—"What is it supposed to mean, that one thing [*Sache*] describes another?" (Heidegger 2008, 48)—by defining science as "imagination in the service of the verifiable truth," and admitting that, "imagination is actually dependent on consciousness. Science itself is so dependent" (Edelman 2006, 8).

In addition, Edelman rejects a computer-based model of mind because brains do not work by using set protocols or algorithms to process data from unambiguous input. Brains process complex and ambiguous sensory and kinesthetic information retroactively, through a range of neuronal responses that "compete" to efficiently and effectively (though not necessarily accurately) process the input (Edelman 2006, 21). The best way of understanding consciousness is not, for Edelman, by analogy with computers, but rather by analogy with how the immune system responds to foreign bodies by "selecting" and reproducing immune cells that effectively combat the danger, a view he calls "neural Darwinism." Moreover, in Edelman's view, brains are unlike computers in that they are not hardware and not context neutral. The development and function of the brain are dependent on the specific life history of the organism and the environmental context in which the organism exists.

Edelman's theory of how the biology of the brain produces conscious experience, while somewhat nonstandard in the field, has several points in its favor from a scientific perspective. First, his account is based on a unique depth of understanding of human embryology and the immune system (the work for which he won a Nobel Prize). Secondly, since the perceptual-motor system (mediated by the brain) and the immune system are the two ways in which our bodies interact with the environment, a principle of evolutionary parsimony supports the idea that the same basic principle might govern both.

Finally, his views appear to be supported by the creation in his lab of "Darwin machines," which use selection-based perceptual and motor systems to identify and remember features of their environment without programming or instruction beyond "preferences" comparable to basic biological needs. The one I saw in action at Edelman's research institute vaguely resembled R2D2 and was able to move among blocks with different colors, textures, and shapes to identify those it considered to "taste" good. These are not traditional robots designed to have artificial intelligence and act like humans but which could, for all that, still be zombies; they are machines designed to develop some level of consciousness based on how that is done by living things. How successful they are remains to be seen, but the project is intriguing.

For all these reasons, I consider the work of Edelman and his associates to be as close as neurobiology is currently able to come to a viable scientific account of consciousness. To make the limits of that account clear, however, note that Edelman supports a version of epiphenomenalism, a close cousin of the spandrel theory cited in the introduction (Edelman 2006, 92).[1]

Edelman's account of how the brain or immune system works is Darwinian through and through, from the macro-level of the evolution of species to the micro-level of how lymphocytes or neuronal pathways develop. Those organisms, systems, or elements of systems that interact most effectively with the environment (where "effectively" is defined in terms of ensuring the survival of the individual or species) will be selected; those that do not will fall by the wayside. This implies, in turn, that multiple options are available at all levels of the population—including random mutations at the level of the organism, adaptive B and T cells in the immune system, and a variety of potential neural pathways in the brain. These options are then selected among based on how well they meet the underlying needs of the organism.

The feature possessed by the brain that is lacking at the other two levels is what Edelman calls "reentry." This refers to the fact that neural pathways in the brain run through the thalamocortical system, which connects the pathways with each other and with the areas of the brain that regulate physical well-being. According to this concept, reentry coordinates the firing of neuronal groups to allow the organism to respond in maximally adaptive ways to its constantly changing environment. Reentry also helps the brain to categorize similar inputs that initiate similar responses, ultimately allowing us to learn. The parallel concept in immunology would be if T cells had a central point of contact through which they could recognize the common features of various forms of the influenza virus and develop a single response for all of them, rather than having to recognize and respond to each variant individually. With higher-order consciousness, the reentry process "bootstraps" itself up to increasingly general and abstract groupings, culminating in the socially shared categories created by human language.[2]

In addition, brain organization exhibits "degeneracy," by which Edelman means that different structures can produce the same outcome. This has two implications. First, no one structure is required to produce a particular response. Neural pathways related to both the written word "stop" and the perception of red octagons will prompt a driver's foot to press down on the brake pedal. Because these two pathways each have their own associations, however, they are woven into different larger webs, which may link red with danger or lead graffiti artists to stencil the word "war" on the sign. Thus, the second implication of degeneracy is that, given higher consciousness and language, it creates the possibility of metaphor and, by extension, literature and other creative arts.

Even in primary, or animal, consciousness, these lateral linkages between neural pathways create what Edelman calls a "scene," a diffuse perceptual and behavioral relationship to the organism's immediate environment that allows it to move purposefully through its world. A well-trained guide dog deciphers neither the word "stop" nor the shape of the stop sign, but rather the shape of the street corner, the presence or absence of moving cars, and the signals transmitted by its human (through touch, sound, or sight) to determine whether to stop or proceed. In both primary and higher-level consciousness, the brain, Edelman points out, operates "not by logic but rather by pattern recognition," trading precision for a wider functional range (Edelman 2006, 58). As a result, the "diverse repertoires" of selectional systems such as the brain and immune system, "are never perfect matches to the contents of the domains they must recognize." Nevertheless, they can be fine-tuned to be more accurate with continued selection, as a dog can be trained to hear approaching cars it cannot see (Edelman 2006, 83). Science happens, according to Edelman, when these refinements in higher-level consciousness are further constrained by "logic, mathematics, and controlled observations" (Edelman 2006, 91).

Logic and science play a secondary role here, however. Edelman, like Heidegger, notes that logic may be a cultural product (Edelman 2006, 96–97). Furthermore, his Darwinism requires the subordination of the theoretical to the practical. His definition of thought implies that it "reflects the activity of sensorimotor brain circuits in which the motoric elements are paramount but do not eventuate in action." Thinking one word while typing another, for example, often results in typing the thought word rather than the intended one, because the "motoric" correlate of a word is the act of typing it. According to his view, thought is not speaking to oneself, as philosophy usually suggests; rather it is aimed at action (as is the spoken word in its own sphere) and is only secondarily cut off from it. (Edelman 2006, 103).[3] Thought is inherently about things—that is, it is intentional, because it is based on perceptual categories that are necessarily categories of things. In another analogy with Heidegger, Edelman rejects a representational theory of truth. For him, "truth is not a given, it is a value that must be worked for" (Edelman 2006, 150–51). He concludes that "although scientific theory is necessarily underdetermined, it is as good as we can get" (Edelman 2006, 156–57).

Which leaves us where? Edelman believes that the relationship between body and mind is analogous to the relationship between the biochemical properties of blood and its redness—"neural action in the core [of the brain] *entails* consciousness, just as the spectrum of the hemoglobin in your blood is entailed by the quantum mechanical structure of that molecule." In other words, the iron content of blood appears, and can be measured, as redness (Edelman 2006, 40). Things that work like *that* will have *this* property, which is not part of their causal power but is nonetheless inseparable from it. This sounds a bit like the spandrel theory discussed in chapter 1. However, Edelman rejects the possibility that all behavior could be nonconscious in the sense that the automatic behavior sometimes seen in cases of epilepsy is nonconscious. He reminds us that such behavior (e.g., driving a car or playing a musical piece on the piano) must first have been learned as a conscious activity. This consideration would rule out all three sorts of philosophical zombies noted by Robinson et al. (2015) because it implies that entirely nonconscious beings could not duplicate the behavior of conscious ones, at least so far as learned behavior is concerned (Edelman 2006, 40). Edelman would reject the possibility of zombies because he believes that, although "the underlying neural activity is what drives individual and mental responses," consciousness "serves to inform us of our brain states and is thus central to our understanding."

The main difference between Robinson et al. and Edelman seems to be the depth of detail to which each takes their epiphenomenalism. If the underlying phenomenon is taken to be behavioral, philosophical zombies and green blood are possible. If it is taken to be neurobiological, consciousness would not be epiphenomenal in the sense that it "does nothing." Rather, it would be, like the redness that corresponds to the chemical structure of hemoglobin, a marker that reflects the underlying physical process. In this consideration, consciousness is, as Edelman says, "one of a number of useful illusions" that apprise us of our physiological state (Edelman 2006, 92).

II: What Neurophenomenology Can't Do

Edelman would have been one of the first to admit that his neurobiological account fails to explain how all the brain mechanisms he describes "*cause* consciousness," as John Searle pointed out in a review of two of Edelman's books (Searle 1995, 56; his emphasis). More recent work in "neurophenomenology," a term introduced by F. J. Varela, seeks to address what Thompson, Lutz, and Cosmelli refer to as an "explanatory gap" between brain science and lived experience (2005, 40–41). In fact, Thompson and his associates cite one of Edelman's co-authored books as an example of work on the neural correlates of consciousness at the beginning of their introduction to neurophenomenology for "neurophilosophers"—that is, analytic philosophers who work on the margins between neurobiology and philosophy. Neurophenomenology allies itself with cognitive science research that, like Edelman's, assumes that "cognitive structures emerge from … recurrent sensorimotor couplings of body, nervous system, and environment" (Thompson, Lutz, and Cosmelli 2005, 42). Walter Freeman has labeled this concept "the 'activist-pragmatist' view of the brain" (Thompson, Lutz, and Cosmelli 2005, 44).

As the name "neurophenomenology" implies, this school of thought draws on phenomenology for its philosophical grounding, especially the work of Edmund Husserl and Maurice Merleau-Ponty. It's primarily scientific emphasis, however, is clear: "Of particular concern to neurophenomenology is the process whereby implicit, unthematized, and intransitively lived-through aspects of experience can become thematized and verbally described, and thereby made available in the form of intersubjective, first-person data for neuroscientific research on consciousness" (Thompson, Lutz, and Cosmelli 2005, 59). The authors further note that phenomenologically, while "the *object* of my perceptual experience … is intersubjectively accessible," the "*perceptual experience* …, on the other hand, is given directly only to me" (Thompson, Lutz, and Cosmelli 2005, 53). It would seem to follow that whatever about my perceptual experience is made available through the process they suggest would no longer *be* my perceptual experience, but rather an account of it for others.

Further, the process of making lived experience explicit for neurobiological research would seem to produce only *correlations* between brain states and consciousness, not "causal" links between them. Thompson and colleagues also tend to make what might be called category mistakes by describing neurological processes in mentalist terms. For example, they write, "To say that a mental-cognitive state is a neural 'interpretation' of current neural activity means that distributed and local neural events are never taken at face value but are always 'seen' or 'evaluated' from the point of view of the assembly most dominant at the time" (Thompson, Lutz, and Cosmelli 2005, 66). That explanation attributes vision, values, and interpretative skills to a group of brain cells. It is hard to imagine how the sentence could be reworded to convey the same meaning without the metaphorical use of consciousness-related words. In addition, it is interesting that the authors resort to the Husserlian *epoché* and describe "the experiencing process, rather than the specific object of experience" in order to disclose "the invariant structures and factors within and across different types of experience" (Thompson, Lutz, and Cosmelli 2005, 70).

There are also scientific issues with the Thompson, Lutz, and Cosmelli research, which is based on only four subjects (Thompson, Lutz, and Cosmelli 2005, 76). For example, "Apart from these patterns common to all subjects, it was also found that the precise topography, frequency, and time course of the synchrony patterns during the preparation period varied widely across subjects" (Thompson, Lutz, and Cosmelli 2005, 8). Edelman's work would lead us to expect such a result, but it is not helpful in the search for a way to close the causal gap between brain states and consciousness. In the end, Thompson, Lutz, and Cosmelli actually disavow Varela's goal of closing the gap. Instead, they seek "to *bridge* the gap by establishing dynamic reciprocal constraints between subjective experience and neurobiology," for which neurophenomenology may have "proposed a clear scientific research program" (Thompson, Lutz, and Cosmelli 2005, 89) but not a philosophical one.

Alva Noë makes a more philosophical application of phenomenological principles to the problem of the neural correlates of consciousness. He argues for what he calls "the Extended Substrate thesis," which holds that "experiences are neural processes, to be sure; but they are not *only neural* processes." This thesis contrasts with a view he calls "Narrow Substrate," which holds that experiences are nothing more than brain events (Noë 2007, 457). Noë argues that "it is only in terms of non-neural features that we can explain how experience has the character that it does"—a concept he calls "Explanatory Externalism" (Noë 2007, 459). Drawing on neuroplasticity (the feature of brain processes Edelman calls "degeneracy"), Noë points out that the visual system is defined not by brain location or neural connections, but by being the brain processes related to sight. Thus, sight is "a function, not a physical notion." However, sight is connected not only to the sensory periphery "driven by" the eyes, but also to the objects seen. Hence, this is an externalist, interactionist view of mental processes: "the substrate of experience needs to be modeled in terms of relations between *three* mappings, not two. In addition to the mapping between the sensory periphery and cortex and the mapping between cortex and experience, we need to take into consideration the mapping between the distal object and the sensory periphery" (Noë 2007, 461–63).

Relying on the same Darwinism as Edelman, Noë points out that "the brain enables us to lock onto, track, and engage with the environment around us. Experience is what we call that involvement with environment. Experience is brain and world involving" (Noë 2007, 465). Furthermore, he claims that this view "challenges the sharp distinction that is accepted between epistemology and metaphysics or ontology" because, in effect, we would never be able to doubt specific claims if we did not know how to make sense of our experience in general as a basis for judging truth.

Noë also rejects the "Dream Argument" for the Narrow Substrate theory of consciousness. That argument asserts that in dreams nothing but brain states are involved, but that the lived experience is indistinguishable from waking experience. He argues instead that in a strictly phenomenological sense, experience "could not occur in the absence of situations and things." This view follows from the fact that dreams and waking experiences are not phenomenologically identical (though they may be confused under certain circumstances), as well as from our evolutionary history. Noë adds the fairly obvious fact that, in parallel with the zombielike behavior discussed by Edelman, "There is probably reason to believe that what we can experience in a dream is limited by our past experience of the world." That means that dreams, like the automatic responses of some epileptic episodes, assume a previous state of conscious interaction with the external world (Noë 2007, 471–72). In another parallel with Edelman, Noë explains the co-prescence or presence as absence of unseen sides of an object in terms of their accessibility to us through our skillful interaction with the world (Noë 2009). And such skillful interaction is, in fact, the direction Edelman and his associates have taken their Darwin machines.[4]

Noë's argument against internalist accounts of consciousness, especially as they have been enshrined in attempts to develop artificial intelligence (AI), echoes Dreyfus's earlier critique of AI. I will discuss Dreyfus's reading of Heidegger later, but here I would like to draw on his *What Computers Can't Do* and more recent articles on cognitive neuroscience to show the limits of the AI enterprise. I maintain that the argument in Dreyfus's book can be devastatingly summarized in two key statements. One, which he attributes to Wittgenstein, is that "whenever human behavior is analyzed in terms of rules, these rules must always contain a *ceteris paribus* condition, that is, they apply 'everything else being equal,' and what 'everything else' and 'equal' means in any specific situation can never be fully spelled out without a regress." This idea leads to the so-called "frame problem" in AI, which appeared in Thompson, Lutz, and Cosmelli (2015) as the challenge of thematizing the unthematized aspects of conscious experience (i.e., what makes "all else" "equal" in any given case). The same problem is implied by Noë as part of his externalist account. Unlike Thompson and Noë, however, Dreyfus emphasizes the social aspects of the elements implicit in our experience—the elements that depend on our existence in a social world that appears to us as meaningful. He notes that "the *ceteris paribus* condition points to a background of practices which are the condition of the possibility of all rulelike activity" (Dreyfus 1979, 56–57). Just as Noë emphasizes that we cannot explain our experiences without taking into account their context, Dreyfus emphasizes that we cannot experience anything as meaningful, and hence explainable, without taking into account our *social* context.

The social world provides our conscious experience with a layer of what Edelman calls "values" beyond the level necessary for bare survival. "Values," in Edelman's sense, explain why we choose one option over another, why we do one thing rather than another. Edelman's Darwin machines are not programmed with goals—as is done in most AI research—but with nontransitive "preferences" for certain "perceptual stimuli" (i.e., blocks of different shapes and colors). The hope is that these machines will build up a repertoire of self-directed behaviors based on those preferences, just as babies learn to reach for a bottle. As babies grow into toddlers, however, much more comes into play in the implicit background of their explicit conscious states. They learn to want smiles as well as food, to enjoy being told stories, to tell stories, to be read to, and to read. These are desires that reach beyond mere survival and make our lives human, but they are also dependent on the social world and, in the case of reading, a social world in which the written word exists. Reading is not just a value for us as individuals; it is valued in our shared social reality, which helps to give us a motivation to read. Not all the facets of that motivation can be thematized for neurophenomenological analysis or captured in a computer program. What ultimately moves us is external to consciousness and not part of our experience, but its source. This is Dreyfus' second key argument in *What Computers Can't Do*: "It is only because our interests are *not* objects in our experience that they can play this fundamental role of organizing our experience into meaningful patterns or regions" (Dreyfus 1979, 274, his emphasis).

More recently, Dreyfus engaged with "Heideggerian AI." He has argued that, in the same vein as Edelman's "values," readiness-to-hand is not, for Heidegger, "a predefined type of situation that triggers a predetermined response" but "a solicitation that calls forth a flexible response to the *significance* of the current situation." That is, the response is geared to a desired outcome. An unready-to-hand nail that sticks out from a closet wall could call for Heidegger's ubiquitous hammer, or it could emerge as an object on which to hang belts. Either of these choices might be made without conscious deliberation, depending on the specifics of the situation. "*Being-in-the-world*," Dreyfus tells us, "is more basic than *thinking* and solving problems; it is not representational at all" (Dreyfus 2007, 254, his emphasis). He suggests that Heideggerian AI might best develop in the direction of Walter Freeman's work, incorporating both Heidegger's and Merleau-Ponty's accounts of being-in-the-world. That concept shares many features with Edelman's model: a behavioral-perceptual intentional arc, holism, learning, and pattern selection (Dreyfus 2007, 257–62). However, Dreyfus concludes that even this optimal model fails to capture our lived experience because it lacks "a model of our particular way of being embedded and embodied such that what we experience is significant for us in the particular way it is." (Dreyfus 2007, 265). Thus, we are left in the same place where Edelman left us—without a way to explain the relationship between brain states and conscious experience.

III: (Almost) Understanding Consciousness and the Limits of Panpsychism

Max Velmans' *Understanding Consciousness* provides the model of the psychological side of cognitive science here because it bridges the gaps between the philosophy of mind and the findings of neuroscience. It also demonstrates a sophisticated understanding of the philosophical literature, most relevantly in the phenomenological tradition.[5] The conclusion of Velmans' book indicates why his ideas are relevant to Heidegger's rethinking of mind and matter, subject and object:

> [W]ho can doubt that our bodies *and* our experience are an integral part of the universe? And who can doubt that each one of us has a unique, conscious perspective on the larger universe of which we are a part? In this sense, we participate in a process by which the universe observes itself—and the universe becomes both the subject and the object of experience. Consciousness and matter are intertwined in mind. Through the evolution of matter, consciousness is given form. And through consciousness, the material universe is *realised*. (Velmans 2009, 351, his emphasis)

The same quotation also reveals, however, the persistent dualism of "bodies" and "experience" that persists in Velmans' thought, as well as his move toward panpsychism.

Among other theories that Velmans considers is one that has strong resonances with Heidegger's ideas. Velmans attributes this "neutral monism" to thinkers as varied as William James, Ernst Mach, and Bertrand Russell. According to Velmans, neutral monists believe that "mental events and physical ones are ... simply different ways of *construing* the world as perceived." Velmans supports this view by noting that "what we observe in the world is neither intrinsically mental nor physical. Rather, we *judge* what we experience to be 'mental' or 'physical' depending on the network of relationships under consideration." While Velmans acknowledges the importance of this "simple (often neglected) point," he argues that "one needs a lot more than this to solve the mind-body problem. For example, one still has to relate the phenomenal world to the very different world described by physics." He also questions how we can be "neutral" about the specific contents of consciousness—that is, "images, dreams, emotions, and thoughts" (Velmans 2009, 32–33). Such a difficulty arises, however, only if one starts with dualism and works backwards, as Velmans most often does, rather than starting with lived experience and moving outward, as I argue Heidegger suggests.

Despite his scientific starting point, Velmans rejects reductionist accounts of consciousness insofar as they suggest the nonexistence of conscious phenomena. He considers "non-eliminative reductionism," but argues that while consciousness may be correlated with, or caused by, brain states, that does not in itself prove that it *is* nothing more than brain states because "*correlation* and *causation* do not establish *ontological identity*" (Velmans 2009, 45; his emphasis). He next considers "emergentism" or "non-reductive physicalism" as an example of dual-property theories—that is, the position that what can be looked at one way as neural activity can be looked at another way as, for example, seeing a tree. Velmans notes, however, that such conversations quickly become linguistic, focusing on "how the terms should be used" and points out that "*relabeling* consciousness ... doesn't really close the gap between 'objective' brains and 'subjective' experiences" (Velmans 2009, 50). Drawing on the psychological and philosophical literature, along with research in artificial intelligence, he concludes that "it is inappropriate to *choose between* first-person [phenomenological] and third-person [scientific] accounts of the mind. A complete psychology requires *both*" (Velmans 2009, 112; his emphasis, my interpolation).

This commitment draws Velmans's account close to the view I attribute to Heidegger. Velmans notes, for example, that "physical objects and events as perceived are *part of* the content of consciousness," suggesting a "broader ontology" for the mind/body duality parallel to the way "electromagnetism ... encompasses" electrical and magnetic phenomena (Velmans 2009, 146–47; his emphasis). Magnetism is not electric, nor is electricity magnetic. Rather, the two phenomena name a set of interrelated properties that describes the nature and behavior of certain things in the world. Velmans believes that mental and physical properties can similarly be invoked in a unified psychology to explain the lived experiences and behaviors of humans. In terms reminiscent of Edelman, Velmans states, "What we normally think of as 'space' also refers, at least in the initial instance, to the phenomenal space that we experience [and] through which we appear to move" (Velmans 2009, 167). Later, he notes that "*what we take to be 'normal perceived reality' has more to do with what enables successful interaction with the world than any immutable, one-to-one mapping of the events described by physics into events-as-perceived*" (Velmans 2009, 190; his emphasis).

Velmans concludes that "if there *were* no human beings and there were no other creatures with perceptual processes similar to human beings, then the world *as we perceive it* would literally cease to be" (Velmans 2009, 194, his emphasis). He acknowledges the Kantian side to his thought, but adds that "unlike Kant, I will argue that the thing itself is knowable, albeit imperfectly," presumably based on the pragmatic focus of our knowledge of the word (Velmans 2009, 174, n 3). He also maintains Kant's ontological dualism—"While the world we experience is a representation that depends for its existence on human perceptual processing, the reality it represents does not" (Velmans 2009, 195). He attempts to evade the paradoxes of representational realism by arguing that experimental science allows us to dig deeper than everyday perception, not to get closer to "reality" but to better "explain, control and predict observable phenomena" (Velmans 2009, 198). Velmans suggests that we can improve the accuracy of our knowledge claims by the twenty-first-century equivalent of Descartes's claim that "being able almost always to avail myself of many of [my senses] in order to examine one particular thing, and, besides that, being able to make use of my memory in order to connect the present with the past ... I ought no longer to fear that falsity may be found in matters every day presented to me by my senses" (Descartes 1976, 198; my interpolation).

Velmans takes this Cartesian position because his residual dualism leads him to believe that the "many differences between the phenomenal world ... and the world described by natural science" imply that "unless one is prepared to reject natural science, one must reject the view that the world simply is as it appears to be" (Velmans 2009, 199). I argue that this is a false dilemma based on the assumption that the world can be only one way and, implicitly, that science is the only reasonable arbiter of that way. At the same time, Velmans is willing to move from objectivity to a form of intersubjectivity that can be both self-critical and critical of alternative intersubjectivities based on "their ability to *fulfill* the purposes for which they are to be used" (Velmans 2009, 216, his emphasis). This intersubjectivity is based on the fact that through language the data lived experience provides us with can be made "potentially public, intersubjective and repeatable," (Velmans 2009, 221). The problem for Velmans as a psychologist is that "there is something deeply mysterious about how activities in brain cells [which he takes as a given, fixed reality] could possibly 'produce' conscious experiences" (Velmans 2009, 266; my interpolation). His basic argument against various forms of physicalism is that they must paradoxically assume the reality of conscious experience in order to know "what it is that they need to eliminate, reduce, or otherwise explain away" (Velmans 2009, 292). Moreover, any physicalist account of consciousness must acknowledge that "third-person scientific accounts are *also* representations" (Velmans 2009, 344, his emphasis), not mechanical reproductions of what is the case.

Velmans' own solution to the problem of consciousness is what he calls "reflexive monism," which recognizes that "the contents of consciousness are both *produced by* initiating entities, events, and processes [in the world] ... and *represent* those entities, events, and processes." He suggests that "overall this [the reflexive model] may be thought of as a biologically useful model of a universe that is described in a very different way by modern physics." Echoing Edelman, Velmans concludes that our experienced world is "an illusion created by the brain, but still, a most useful one" (Velmans 2009, 296–97; my interpolations). His "monist" account of this illusion, however, is a form of panpsychism that he describes as the assumption that "there must be some thing, event, or process that one can know in two complimentary ways." It is not a dual property theory, but a dual existence theory based on ontological monism and epistemological dualism, again on the model of electromagnetic phenomena, which are one thing known by two different sets of properties (Velmans 2009, 309). In this view, "first- and third-person accounts of the mind are *complementary and mutually irreducible*" (Velmans 2009, 173, his emphasis). Velmans also cites the work of Alfred North Whitehead as "anticipating" his own model (Velmans 2009, 131).

Velmans expresses a preference for a panpsychist "continuity theory" to explain both where consciousness comes from and what it does (Velmans 2009, 343). A discontinuity theory assumes that at some point in Earth's history increasingly complex organic molecules evolved into the first rudimentary living things. Eons later, at some point in the evolutionary process, brains became sufficiently complex that consciousness appeared as an entirely new and unique phenomenon. Velmans argues that discontinuity theorists have difficulty pinpointing the state of development at which these monumental transformations occurred, as well as the ways in which the transformations came about.[6] Continuity theorists, by contrast, believe that life and consciousness have always existed, from "the birth of the universe," and they merely became more complex and more apparent as time progressed. In addition to solving the problem of the genesis of life and consciousness, continuity theories, according to Velmans, solve the problem of the causal relationship between brain states and mental states. As previously noted, these states are not causally related at all, but are two sides of the same phenomenon (Velmans 2009, 342–43). Thus, while Velmans takes the conversation about mind/body dualism about as far as it can go within the confines of cognitive science, his conclusions rise and fall with the viability of a panpsychist account.

Velmans is not the only major contemporary theorist to move in the direction of panpsychism. Philosopher Elizabeth Grosz, for example, draws on the work of Henri Bergson, Gilles Deleuze, Félix Guattari, Gilbert Simondon, and

Raymond Ruyer to trace a continuous line from inorganic matter through plant and animal life to human consciousness. In her view, "Life does not add a vital spark to the inertia of the inorganic." Rather, she argues, "Matter in all its complex forms contains life; and life always pushes matter's possibilities for being otherwise to the maximum." Grosz further argues that purely material events, such as storms, have "a strange kind of life." One can also see this in traffic on a freeway, which flows in much the same way that fluids flow through a tube. In addition, Grosz notes that matter has self-organizing principles (e.g., the forces that structure the atom, magnetism, gravity) that allow it to respond and adapt to changes in the "chaos" around it. At an evolutionary step up, we find plants that react to and interact with the material world, even displaying a kind of material memory. This observation leads Deleuze and Guattari to propose, "The plant … is on its way to a new kind of brain." For Grosz, all types of life, even plants, have some form of consciousness, a form of interiority, an inside to be protected from a potentially harmful outside—and they solve problems at some level (Grosz 2011, 20–23). I suspect that the basic motivation for all these thinkers may be the desire for a less bifurcated and more respectful and circumspect attitude toward the planet and the natural world—an attitude that might undo the disastrous ecological effects of human-centric arrogance. This dynamic version of a continuity theory, however, still relies, as does Velmans' more traditional view, on the categories and presuppositions of modern techno-science. For that reason, it fails to provide an adequate solution to the ecological problems and other complications that scientism and dualism have created.

I would argue that the move toward panpsychism as a solution to the mind/body problem is unnecessary if we seriously consider Heidegger's insights about how to rethink both the psychic and the physical rather than attempting to join them together. Panpsychism suffers from three defects that prevent it from being the strong alternative to the ideology of technological modernity—an alternative that we need to save the world and perhaps ourselves. The first defect is that the sole motivation for panpsychism seems to be the absence of any other solution to the mind/body problem. We experience material bodies and our own phenomenal states, but we have no way to reconcile those two entities into a unified theory of embodied human life. Consciousness does not have a place in the world of modern science. Rather than seeing this as a *reductio ad absurdum* of the scientific understanding of the world, Velmans points to the fact that the creation of consciousness is no more mysterious than the creation of the physical universe. In this view, consciousness—or something like it—has always been part of the universe. Looking at plants or the ocean, we might see that this idea has a certain initial plausibility. But looking at a piece of chalk, I would argue, it has none. It is one thing to suggest that inanimate objects have structure, limits, and a dynamic of their own, but it is a different thing to say that they have some form of proto-phenomenal experience. They have an inside and an outside that may protect the inside, but that does not mean they have anything like consciousness. The ancient Greeks believed that trees and water could be occupied by dryads and naiads, which caused their sometimes human-like behaviors, but these behaviors were never taken to be signs of consciousness in the natural objects themselves.

The second problem with panpsychism is the extent to which it relies on modern techno-science and remains dualistic at its core. Consciousness may have been present in the physical world all along, but it remains distinct from and irreconcilable with the physical world. Why is this? Near the beginning of the modern age, Spinoza offered a more thorough "continuity" theory. In *The Ethics*, he takes seriously Descartes's concepts of "substance" and "infinity" and defines God as "an absolutely infinite being; that is, a substance consisting of infinite attributes" (Spinoza 1982, 31). For Spinoza, mind and body are only two of those attributes—the two ways of experiencing the world that we, as finite beings, have available to us: "thinking substance and extended substance are one and the same substance, comprehended now under this attribute [of God], now under that" (Spinoza 1982, 67; my interpolation). Spinoza gives no examples of the other attributes of God (not surprisingly, since we have no access to them), but we could imagine a third way of knowing the nature of God that we might call, borrowing from Spinoza's background in optics and geometry, "mathematical." One of the lasting paradoxes of the modern period is that mathematics is a deductive system, a product of pure consciousness that "works" in the empirical world. Enough mathematicians (and philosophers) claim to experience the world in a purely mathematical way to provide us with a vague outline of Spinoza's third way of knowing the infinite attributes of God. This possibility underscores the difference between the dualism inherent in a panpsychist account dependent on a concept of *psyche* and its purported opposite, and a pantheistic account that undercuts Descartes's dualism entirely.

Ultimately, however, the most basic problem with panpsychism is that it does not solve the problem of how mind and body are related. Velmans believes there are no nonarbitrary criteria by which to choose between continuity theories and discontinuity theories, but he finds panpsychism to be more "elegant" (Velmans 2009, 343). His conclusion is that "consciousness and matter are intertwined in the mind" (Velmans 2009, 351)—a claim with which Edelman, Noë, Grosz, and the others would agree, but one that explains nothing. If the existence of consciousness at the "macro" level of human brains is scientifically inexplicable, a panpsychist account merely moves the problem back in time to the moment when the first proto-conscious/proto-physical entity appeared. Why did matter appear in the history of the cosmos with the potential for consciousness inherent in it? Note that this is a question of a different type than the parallel physicalist question about the origins of life, where the answer can be parsed out in terms of atoms, carbon molecules, and other chemical explanations. The panpsychist question is already dualist—that is, why and how did both physical and mental potentialities arise? What happened in the "Big Bang" is mysterious, but one mystery cannot be used to solve another. Rather, panpsychism compounds the mystery by asking science to answer a question that it does not possess the tools to address.

Velmans has proven that if the basic problem is the relationship between our phenomenal experience and the scientific account of the world, it cannot be solved by eliminating the phenomenal side of the relationship, as the reductive accounts attempt to do. Even Edelman's epiphenomenalism can be seen as reductive at the extremes. Consciousness is real for all of the views discussed here. More importantly, it is not a spandrel. It makes a difference in the world. It matters. However, neuroscientists cannot tell us what consciousness *is* or how it is "caused" by the physical reality they take as given. Hence, we return to the more primordial understanding of consciousness that I believe guided Heidegger's thought from beginning to end.

Notes

1. More specifically, Robinson and his colleagues' spandrel theory argues that their view is compatible both with epiphenomenalism and with its denial, but that epiphenomenalism entails the truth of the spandrel account (Robinson, Maley, and Piccinini 2015, 176). https://www.researchgate.net/publication/282619766_Is_Consciousness_a_Spandrel

2. For a complete account of this process, see Edelman's (1987). *Neural Darwinism.*

3. Cf. Derrida's (1976) *Of Grammatology.*

4. Cf. Heidegger's (2010) *Logic: The Question of Truth*, pp. 84–85.

5. I owe a debt of gratitude to the late Patrick Heelan, who directed me to Velmans' work, and to my former student, Michael Heraly, whose excitement about Velmans' ideas prompted the conversations that produced the first glimmerings of this book.

6. In *The Remembered Present* and elsewhere, Edelman (1989) claims to have solved both these problems. I will leave it to the reader to gauge his success.

3 The Earliest Vision

Something non-material…but also not unmaterial

—Martin Heidegger (*Toward a Definition of Philosophy*, 2008)

I: Towards a Definition of Philosophy

Approaching Heidegger from the perspective of the mind/body problem, it is disconcerting to find him directly asking the question, "*What is the psychic?*" in the 1919 lectures translated as *Towards the Definition of Philosophy* (Heidegger 2008, 47; his emphasis).[1] The standard reading of the relationship between the mental (as psyché) and the natural world (as physis) in these and other early lectures relates them to intentionality.[2] I believe, however, that such a reading overemphasizes the aspects of Heidegger's thought most closely related to Husserl's work and to the technological understanding of nature and human experience. Furthermore, such a reading underemphasizes the extent to which these lectures represent a new and unique vision. Heidegger's observation in these lectures about Wilhelm Windelband—"I cannot make Windelband's account more intelligible that he has himself" (Heidegger 2008, 115)—can also be applied to this early phase of Heidegger's own thought. My goal is to make at least a prima facie argument that what Heidegger was undertaking here, and what brought him such notoriety among his students and peers, was more than a new account of intentionality or a preview of *Being and Time*. Rather, it was a much more radical project.[3]

Early in the 1919 lectures, Heidegger notes, "We are now no longer posing the question [of what the psychic/mental is] in relation to a specific region of Being [i.e., psychology]…since everything either *is* psychic or is mediated *through* the psychic." He is referring to psychology in a purely descriptive sense here, but the problem lies in the relationship between the mental as something that is described and the mental as something that generates the description. If the mental is just another sort of thing, "What is it supposed to mean, that one thing [*Sache*] describes another?" In a preview of themes we will see in later works, such as "What is Metaphysics?" (1931), he notes, "Is there even a single thing when there are only things? Then there would be no thing at all; not even *nothing*, because with the sole supremacy of the sphere of things there is not even the 'there is' [*es gibt*]" (Heidegger 2008, 47–48; his emphasis, translator's interpolations).

If minds are identical with brains, and if the mental is either epiphenomenal or part of the physical world, then consciousness loses its specific quality as mental—that is, as consciousness. Things as things cannot be "there" for a consciousness if minds are merely one kind of object among others, determined by the same laws and understood by the same methods.[4] In that case, all that would exist would be "stuff" in various configurations, behaving in ways that could not even be thought of as law-like, because there would be no consciousness to recognize the laws. Robots might observe regularities, but they can never discover laws of nature, for reasons that David Hume has made clear. To return to Heidegger's terms, if there is nothing to which beings are given as the beings they are, would there be any "things" at all?

The next section of these lectures, "Phenomenology as Pre-Theoretical Primordial Science," picks up the same point in terms that link the early lectures to Heidegger's later work on technology. "We stand at an abyss: either into nothingness, that is, absolute reification, pure thingness, or we somehow leap into *another world*, more precisely, we manage for the first time to make the leap [*Sprung*] into the world as such" (Heidegger 2008, 51; his emphasis, translator's interpolation). So we see that already in 1919, it is science—or perhaps more accurately, scientism—that has brought us to this abyss that threatens to cut us off from the world. In this world, as such, "Neither anything physical nor anything psychic is given." Heidegger introduces the concept of questioning comportment here, because the lived experience is not of an "I" who perceives an external "nature," but of an "it lives" and "moreover that it lives toward something." This something toward which "it" lives is not some intentional object that is encountered, but rather what Edelman calls a "value" or a perceived means to such a value. It is a positive and evolutionarily advantageous state, whether it be a full stomach in the case of an animal, a "tasty" block in the case of one of Edelman's Darwin machines, or a human goal such as work/life balance. For Heidegger, such values or goals necessarily create questions about how to achieve them, which, in turn, generate knowledge (e.g., porcupines aren't worth the trouble to eat; pink blocks "taste" good; scheduling time for exercise is part of a healthy life). Thus, "Questioning comportment is motivated, one might say, by the desire to know" (Heidegger 2008, 52–53).[5]

Along with something questionable, lived experience also gives us "that which, just on its own (in respect of questioning and questionability), cannot ultimately be understood. This is its ownmost meaning [*Eigen-sinn*] which it cannot explain by itself." That is, while we can ask questions about the world around us and, to some extent, explain it, we cannot in the same way explain ourselves as questioners. Heidegger notes the possible Husserlian/Cartesian objection that the "there is" (*es gibt*) gives us something "psychic" because it comes back to an "I" in reference to what there is "*for me*." Heidegger's response to this objection is to deny that "the experience has any relation to any individual 'I,'" even if "it belongs to *my* life" (Heidegger 2008, 54–55; his emphasis). He elaborates by making the usual professorial move—he turns to his lectern. When he sees it, "the meaningful is primary and immediately given to me without any mental detours across thing-oriented apprehension." The lectern is not encountered as an object for an "I," but as a "ready-to-hand" thing—a place where anyone can set books and papers, part of a pre-existing world of academic meaning (and one that is shared among all the instructors who use that space). Even someone unfamiliar with the European university, he states, would not see the lectern as a bare object, but as part of a world of meanings, even if the meaning may be unknown. This is because, just as "*es gibt*," there *is* something meaningful: "It is everywhere the case that '*it worlds*' [*es weltet*]" (Heidegger 2008, 58; his emphasis, translator's interpolation).[6]

The three levels of analysis here become fully distinct only in his later thinking, but they can be teased apart even in this early work. The first level is the Edelman/evolutionary level (just noted), which is comparable to Aristotle's understanding of the *telos*, or final cause of all living things. Next is the individual level of my "ownmost meaning," corresponding to my "projects" and goals in life, the specific ways I mediate between my material environment, my biological needs, and my relationships with others like myself. But that mediation can occur only in the context of a social environment that provides a world of meaning within which I and others can make sense of the things around us. The concept of "work/life balance" would have been equally incomprehensible to my grandfather, who worked a nine-to-five white-collar job, and to his farmer forbearers, who worked from sunrise to sunset, despite the disparity in how their lives were in or out of "balance." Thus, I am doubly not a subject in the Cartesian sense. I am not a single thinking thing or pole that exists primordially in relation to specific objects in the world. Instead, I am an active seeker of answers to questions. Furthermore, I am not an individual mind independent of the sociolinguistic world in which I find myself. Rather, I am an active, embodied being whose questions, values, and other ideas are derived from what is available to me in a specific historical time and place.[7]

Heidegger concludes this section by making claims that carry the argument far beyond intentionality. "Lived experience does not pass in front of me like a thing, but I appropriate [*er-eigne*] it to myself, and it appropriates [*er-eignet*] itself according to its essence." This is not a process, he explains, but an occurrence (*ein Ereignis*), because I never see "something thing-like," or "an objectivated sphere of beings, a Being, nor physical or psychical Being" that I then transform into a meaningful world.[8] I see objects already imbued with meanings from which these other ways of understanding them are only later abstracted. The event of appropriation "is not to be taken as if I appropriate the lived experience to myself from outside or from anywhere else; 'outer' and 'inner' have as little meaning here as 'physical' and 'psychical'. The experiences are events of appropriation in so far as they live out of one's 'own-ness', and life lives only in this way." Our experience of the world begins with a question presented as a behavioral-perceptual whole embedded in an already meaningful, pre-personal, social context from which the question arises. Only later—as a result of analysis undertaken for other, no-longer-practical purposes—can such categories as inner/outer, mental/physical, and human/nature be isolated and reified as the abstract individual "elements" of what was initially a seamless and integral event.

Note again that this unitary experience can become the basis for the study of nature, but it cannot itself be the direct object of such study. "How is a science supposed to be built upon this? Science is knowledge and knowledge has objects.... A science of experiences would have to objectify experiences and thus strip away their non-objective character as lived experience" (Heidegger 2008, 60; translator's interpolations). This is the key to the argument. A science of consciousness as consciousness is impossible, not because consciousness exists outside of nature or because it is an epiphenomenon of natural processes, but because once consciousness becomes an object of study, it is no longer consciousness. In a slightly different vocabulary, and with different points of emphasis, George Kovacs declares these lectures to be "an entirely new concept of philosophy that is beyond any relation to the ultimate questions of humanity." Kovacs believes that the early lectures set Heidegger on a path that was not fully realized until "The End of Philosophy and the Task of Thinking" 45 years later.[9]

If we begin with the lived experience, rather than a theoretical attitude, "the opposition between the psychical and the physical [does] not enter our field of view at all, nor [do] any thing-like occurrences" (Heidegger 2008, 77; my interpolation). We are in a pre-scientific, pre-theoretical space. Heidegger considers the objection that such a space cannot exist, because language is already theoretical insofar as it abstracts from lived experience and generalizes it, but he argues that this claim mischaracterizes language. For him, language is "primordially living and experiential." In other words, language itself is part of the world of lived experience, and so we encounter it, in the first place, as a tool to help us navigate in that world. We abstract and generalize not initially to theorize, but for simple practical purposes, as Edelman suggests (Heidegger 2008, 89). This practice not only makes it possible for philosophy to talk about lived experience, but it provides the basis for continuity between pre-theoretical and theoretical uses of language. It also explains "the puzzling presence of determination prior to all theoretical description" because such description is based on our pre-theoretical experience "for which the convenient title of the irrational has been invented" (Heidegger 2008, 89–90).[10] Language—like the world in which we live and the body through which we live in it—is a medium through which we "reckon" with things. It is a non-material materiality that is itself neither a thing nor transparent to thought, but it can be the basis for experiential knowledge (such as the significance of another person's choice of words) that precedes the distinction between the rational and irrational.

Towards the Definition of Philosophy also includes lectures from the summer of 1919 in which Heidegger credits Emil Lask's work with making possible "a harmonizing of science (natural science) and the life of the spirit," while recognizing the need for a "*phenomenological critique* of transcendental philosophy of values" (Heidegger 2008, 94–97; his emphasis).[11] Heidegger follows a strain in Windelband's thought on truth that reappears in his own later work. He reads Windelband as saying, "All propositions of knowledge are already a combination of judgement and evaluation; they are representational connections whose truth-value is decided by affirmation or denial" (Heidegger 2008, 116). Consciousness is irreducible because it relates two "contents" to get "truth" (Heidegger 2008, 122). Without this relation, there is simply a juxtaposition or, at best, a matching of propositions or of propositions and perceptions with no evaluative element.

Heidegger argues that Windelband also believes, "above all, so long as one regards knowledge as representation, an element which necessarily belongs to the concept of knowledge is not present: the knowing subject. For things like representations are objects, and the standpoint of knowledge as representation has to do not with a relation between subject and object, but with a relation between two objects, a relation which becomes quite incomprehensible as knowledge, for a subject is required that ascertains this copying of things by representations— and this knowledge cannot itself be a representation." Heidegger adds that, for Windelband, "the problem is now the judging subject" (Heidegger 2008, 140). This line of thought culminated in the work of Windelband's student (and Lask's teacher), Heinrich Rickert. In terms reminiscent of American Pragmatism, Heidegger reads Rickert as saying that "all assertions about reality" are not "true because they agree with reality, because they assert what really is, but *real* is what is recognized by judgements. The real becomes a species of the true" (Heidegger 2008, 142).[12]

Appendix I of *Towards the Definition of Philosophy* consists of notes by Oskar Becker about a lecture titled, "On the Nature of the University and Academic Study," which was also presented in the summer of 1919. Here, Heidegger engages indirectly with the relationship between philosophy and sciences in terms of "life-experience." He defines this term based on a differentiation between "sciences of explanation" and "sciences of understanding." Needless to say, he aligns philosophy with the latter, but differentiates two kinds of "*experiencedness* [*Erlebtheit*]): 1) lived *experiences* [*gelebte Erlebnisse*] as such; 2) experienced *contents*, that *which* I have experienced." He identifies life-experience with the former, but also with "the historical I," which is always embodied: "The contexture of life-experience is a context of situations which interpenetrate each other. The fundamental character of life-experience is given through the necessary relation to *corporeality*. This is of fundamental significance. '*Sensibility*'...is life-experience." But he also describes it as social: "The practical-historical is necessarily of a *social* nature, it stands in the life-contexture with other I's." The study of "contents," which he seems to identify with "theoretical comportment" (i.e., science), "removes itself from life-experience.... The theoretical world is not always there, but is accessible only in a constantly renewed divesting of the natural world," that is, of abstracting from lived experience (Heidegger 2008, 156–58; his emphasis, translator's interpolations). Thus, a clear subtext in the early lectures is to differentiate philosophy from science and "scientism" in the wartime German university, which raises questions and themes that echo through the whole of Heidegger's career.

II: Phenomenological Interpretations (of Aristotle)

Heidegger's invocation of "life-experience" in the 1919 lectures contrasts sharply with the "Loose Pages" appended to his 1922 lectures on *Phenomenological Interpretations of Aristotle*: "not life, not world, but Being, existence" (Heidegger 2001, 140). We can see him clearly on the path toward *Being and Time* here, which is the path not only away from "life" philosophies and panpsychism, but also away from Husserl. After invoking both Henri Bergson and Rickert in the 1922 lectures, Heidegger comments, "The term, 'life,' is remarkably vague today," and he later adds that "we merely play with the term—or, rather, it is this term that plays with the philosopher" (Heidegger 2001, 62). In his attempt to avoid this trap, Heidegger conceptualizes life and world not as "two separate, self-subsistent Objects," but in such a way that "world is the basic category of the content-sense in the phenomenon, life" (Heidegger 2001, 65). In other words, world is where we encounter things and, correlatively, life is the phenomenal fact of that encounter. Consequently, life disappears as an explanatory term independent of lived experience because, as suggested earlier, it is dependent on the categories of the technological scientism that Heidegger intends to combat. Despite his belief that "we need to read Nietzsche, Bergson" in conjunction with Scheler (Heidegger 2001, 62), Heidegger's conclusion is that "life = existence, '*being*' in and through life" (Heidegger 2001, 64; his emphasis).

Heidegger makes the radical nature of his underlying project clearer in these lectures (not a difficult task, given the murky prose of the ones from 1919). He states that the aim of philosophy must be "the pure cognition of the original questionability, i.e., at the same time, the pure cognition of the labyrinthine basic character of human existence" (Heidegger 2001, 42). He returns to the image of the irrational leap: "a leap into a drifting boat, and it all depends on getting the mainsheet in hand and looking into the wind" (Heidegger 2001, 29). He also returns to the problem of defining philosophy and differentiating it from the sciences: "Why the ever new efforts to raise philosophy finally to the rank of a secure, absolute science?"

In contrast to this, he argues, "Insofar as philosophy delimits itself, its limits do not occur within the region of Being which the sciences divide up among themselves (and it remains questionable whether this dividing up is worth anything!)." Rather than seeing philosophy as the "basic science," he defines it as *"cognitive comportment to beings in terms of Being."* Being is specifically not the most general universal (Heidegger 2001, 43–44; his emphasis)—as he will remind us in future works, including *Being and Time* in 1927 (Heidegger 1962, 22) and *Introduction to Metaphysics* in 1935 (Heidegger 2000, 42). In short, "Philosophy is 'ontology,' indeed, it is radical ontology, and as such is phenomenological" (Heidegger 2001, 46). In response to the move in early twentieth-century philosophy away from metaphysics and toward science, Heidegger makes, already in 1922, the opposite move, from metaphysics to ontology. At the same time, he warns us that philosophy, especially in the context of the university, must avoid Nietzsche's fate and refuse to be "sacrificed on the altar of literature" (Heidegger 201, 50).

Although not truly the focus of these lectures, Aristotle is invoked sufficiently for Heidegger to consider the word "category," which he redefines as primarily interpretative rather than logical: "Categories can be understood only insofar as factical life is compelled to interpretation." In words reminiscent of Edelman's account of how our minds "bootstrap" stimuli into more general and abstract groupings, Heidegger states that the categories are not external impositions on factical life. "They are *alive in life*" and remain viable despite the theoretical "haziness [that] is indebted to life itself; the facticity of life consists in holding to this debt, ever falling into it anew."[13] This view parallels Edelman's awareness that our abstract generalizations come to us rather than being something that we explicitly *do*, and that it is more important for these generalizations to be useful than to be exact representations of "external" reality. As we have seen, pre-theoretical lived experience exists as the implicit (Heidegger prefers "non-explicit") awareness out of which theoretical thinking can emerge. But this thinking must always return to lived experience, both in the sense that the theoretician must, as Hume noted, live a life and in the sense that lived experience serves as a measure of the truth of theories (Heidegger 2001, 65–67; his emphasis; my interpolation).

This hint at themes from *Being and Time* becomes stronger when Heidegger invokes "caring." He states, "Life, as caring, lives in a world" (Heidegger 2001, 70), and he characterizes caring as what gives that world meaning. "I encounter myself in a world which acquires and takes its determinate meaningfulness from my own self, but in which the self 'is' not there *qua* self, and where the 'from my own self' is neither reflectively given nor explicitly placed on stage within this reflection." I do not *decide* to care about the people around me. Rather, they appear to me as entities to be cared about, whether that reaction is natural or learned. The world of caring is an inherently social world, organized around and by other people. "The shared world is encountered in 'part' in one's own world, insofar as a person lives with other people, is related to them in some mode of care, and finds himself in *their* world of care" (Heidegger 2001, 72; his emphasis). The meaningfulness of our shared world exists prior to the objects in that world: "the world is not built up from isolated, objective 'surround-relations' [*Umwelt*; "environment" in *Toward a Definition of Philosophy* and elsewhere] of ordered and to-be-ordered objects in relation to one another." Except in some cases of brain dysfunction, we "see" human needs even if we feel no need to do anything about them. This is because factical life "lives the world as the 'in which' and 'toward which' and 'for which' of life."[14]

In the next of these lectures, Heidegger relates caring back to intentionality and asks, "[D]id intentionality come down from heaven?" His answer is, "In regard to all categorical structures of facticity, intentionality is their basic formal structure." In other words, the "categorical structures of facticity" implicitly have the structure of intentionality as pre-theoretical. Caring is not directed at abstract objects, but at focal points of factical concern. Caring is *per se* pretheoretical: "caring is not intended as an event or occurrence whose presence at hand would be graspable in a simple act of constitution which would need no further determination in its own horizon since it would be related to a reality of a leveled-down experience." Caring is not the right sort of topic for an intentional analysis because it is the source of our "interests" that directs the directedness of our minds. All the same, as we see again in *Being and Time*, caring structures human life. (Heidegger 2001, 96–100).

The effort to ground intentionality in pre-theoretical lived experience is especially interesting in the context of the continuity of Heidegger's thought across his career, because he interweaves the discussion of care in these lectures with the concept of "ruinance" (the English cognate of *die Ruinanz*, from *ruina*, or "collapse"). This neologism foreshadows his later work on both inauthenticity and the dangers of technology, and it may be an attempt to avoid the religious overtones of the language of "falling" and "guilt" he uses in *Being and Time* and other writings. Ruinance is the movement of factical life understood as collapse. This movement is not "caused" by factical life, but rather is the result of the existence of factical life in an "emptiness" that is "the possibility of its movement" (Heidegger 2001, 98). Beyond the fact that one cannot move except into a space that is "empty," this movement is not "intentional" in either sense of the word. Instead, we are drawn forward by the emptiness in a way analogous to the way the collapse of a wall draws the rest of a building toward it and down with it because of the emptiness it creates. Ruinance, however, is not a single event but the constant state of factical life. A better metaphor might be the reverse of lining up dominoes and knocking one over so that they all fall. In ruinance, instead of the first domino falling toward the next one and pushing it, the first domino would fall away from the next one and pull it in its wake because of the emptiness caused by its fall. This would then prompt the rest of the dominoes to move forward in an infinite series. Or consider how air is drawn into the emptiness created by a flash of lightning to generate thunder, but occurs as a continuous process of forward movement.

In another foreshadowing of his future arguments, Heidegger elaborates on the negative side of ruinance in terms of time: "Factical life *has its time*; 'time' which is entrusted to it, which it can 'have' in various ways: to remain in expectation, in safekeeping." In contrast, "Factical, ruinant life, 'has no time,' because its basic movedness, ruinance itself, takes away 'time'." Ruinant, inauthentic life loses itself and its time in the daily rushing after things as it follows the demands made on it by its social/material context.

Conversely, "'to have no time,' as a mode of factical life, expresses its ruinance." This means that ruinance also "seeks to abolish the historiological from facticity," to cut us off from understanding ourselves as historical beings, to separate us from our history and, thus, from understanding ourselves as we truly are. The result is that "care, understood in terms of its actualization, devotes itself to life more and more and ultimately reposes on it; i.e., factical life...becomes in the end, openly or not, frantic over itself and confused." We cannot attend to things we truly care about because we do not know what we truly are; we have lost ourselves in the day-to-day rush of the ruinant world. Heidegger invokes Bergson in this context by noting that "the aforementioned characters of ruinance could easily be taken as fixed basic properties of a being, and thus, posing as fundamental determinations of the existence of life, they could be used to launch an ontological metaphysics of life—e.g., in Bergson's or Scheler's sense. That would be a convenient misunderstanding" (Heidegger 2001, 103–5; his emphasis).

Heidegger's discussion then closes the connection between the emptiness of ruinance and the nothingness of human existence. We fall into ruinance because we exist as beings without a core, as nothings driven to fill up time to hide our nothingness from ourselves. "The 'whereto' of the collapse is not something foreign to it but is itself of the character of factical life and indeed is '*the nothingness of factical life*'." Heidegger already understands that "not every nothingness is identical with every other one, although we might say in a formal argument that 'nothingness' is everywhere and always precisely 'nothing' and 'nothing else!'"[15] He also makes it clear that "'nothingness' must be interpreted in every case on the basis of the respective sense of Being it negates." The absence of another human is not the same as the absence of one's car, nor as the absence of a god in which one once believed.

This idea is the basis for the link between intentionality and nothingness as privation. Ruinance and the distracting "confusion" it causes mean that one's life is encountered "*along with* the lived world and as such a world. The result is that the world thereby acquires the character of opacity and, despite all its immediacy, remains an enigma, at least in its existence itself and in the way it is encountered" (Heidegger 2001, 108–10; his emphasis). Scientifically examining that opaque, ruinant world will never reveal its source or inmost nature. It will also never reveal the nature of the consciousness for whom that world exists. Philosophy's task is to take another path—"genuine questioning consists in living in the answer itself in a searching way, such that the answering maintains a constant relation to the questioning, i.e., such that the latter remains alive, or, in other words, such that the basic experiences retain a factically historiological vitality in factical life and in its ontological sense" (Heidegger 2001, 114). We can see in this quotation the equivocation between Heidegger's views on what philosophy should do ("genuine questioning") and how one should live ("living in the answer itself")—views that will come to a head in *Being and Time* and the later clash with Jean-Paul Sartre over the nature of existentialism.[16]

III: Phenomenological Interpretations (in Connection with Aristotle)

Another Heidegger text from 1922 has a more direct connection to Aristotle, as well as to existentialism. "Phenomenological Interpretations in Connection with Aristotle: An Indication of the Hermeneutical Situation" is the introduction to a unwritten book intended to incorporate Aristotle, "primal Christianity, medieval Scholasticism, and Husserl's phenomenology" into Heidegger's own "historically oriented hermeneutical-phenomenological ontology," according to John van Buren, the editor of the collection in which the text appears (Heidegger 2002c, 8). "The object of philosophical research is human Dasein insofar as it is interrogated with respect to the character of its being," Heidegger writes, adding "life is in such a way that in the concrete temporalizing of its being, it is anxiously concerned about its being, even when it goes out of its way to avoid itself. A characteristic of the being of factical life is that it finds itself hard to bear." Here, "life" is always human life: "the term ζωή, *vita* [life], points to a basic phenomenon that the interpretation of human Dasein in Greek thought, the Old Testament, New Testament Christianity, and Graeco-Christian thought made central." Again, albeit indirectly, science appears as derivative from, and privative relative to, factical life. It is one way of looking at the world among many—"a mere looking around without any view to directing oneself to routine tasks.... The looking becomes more fully actualized when one proceeds to define the world looked at and as such can organize itself into the form of *science*." In this way, the world of science has "been stripped of all significance," though it still provides "the necessary point of departure for epistemological and *ontological* problems" (Heidegger 2002c, 113–17; his emphasis, translator's interpolations).

Heidegger's references to not only Dasein, but also "care," the "with-world," (Heidegger 2002c, 115) "falling," "alienating," "the *'no one'*," "authentic," and "death" (Heidegger 2002c, 118) in this text point forward to *Being and Time*. Much here also points beyond that to his lectures on the ancient Greeks. As we will see, the turn to Aristotle and the Greeks is centered on the concept of truth. "We are told that for Aristotle 'truth' 'occurs in judgment' and is more precisely the 'agreement' of thought with its object," but Heidegger contends that "no trace of the concept of truth as 'agreement,' the common conception of λόγος as valid judgment or, above all, a 'representationalist theory' can be found in Aristotle." In keeping with Heidegger's later emphasis on truth as *alētheia*, he argues here that "Ἀληθεύειν [being true] does not mean 'possessing the truth' but rather taking the *beings* meant in each case and as such into true safekeeping as unveiled." In a strange echo of A. J. Ayer, Heidegger cites Aristotle as saying (*De anima* Γ) that "the expressions 'truth' and 'true' do not really tell us anything" because truth simply presents what is as it is. Falsity, on the other hand, is what results from judgment when we take something *as* something and "the object winds up giving itself out as something it is not" (Heidegger 2002c, 130–31; translator's interpolation).[17]

Because we will spend much of this book discussing truth as a means to understanding the nature of consciousness in Heidegger's writings, it is worth pointing out that the above definitions of truth and falsity articulate with Aristotle's understanding of the difference between what has consciousness (i.e., Dasein) and what does not. Heidegger begins his discussion of this part of *Nicomachean Ethics* (Z 6) by considering the difference between science (*epistēmē*) and practical wisdom (*phronēsis*). There science is presented as "the kind of understanding consisting in a pure and simple looking at … [that] brings into true safekeeping those beings whose 'from-out-of-which' is, as they themselves are, in such a way that it necessarily always is what it is." In other words, science deals with what is fixed and lawlike, the behavior of material things that cannot act otherwise than they do. By contrast, human behavior is not law-like in this way. Nevertheless, human behavior is still rational because it can, through deliberate action, follow the rational principles of practical wisdom, with all the *ceteris paribus* clauses that Aristotle packs into his many invocations of the right time, the right way, and so on.[18] Heidegger continues: "Circumspection with regard to the care for and discussion of human well-being brings into true safekeeping those beings which, along with their 'from-out-of-which,' *can* in themselves *be otherwise*" (Heidegger 2002c, 134; his emphasis)—that is, Dasein. Heidegger follows the thread of *phronēsis* to note that for Aristotle, life as "the with which of dealings"—human life—is "defined simply in a formal manner as capable of being otherwise than it is" (Heidegger 2002c, 136).

Both thinkers pick up this topic elsewhere. Aristotle, in *Metaphysics* (Theta 2), states, "Such sources of change are sometimes in inanimate objects, and sometimes in animate beings; some in any organism's life in general, and others characteristic of a life in so far as it has reason.... Powers with reason have contrary effects, whereas any power without rational control has its specific effects: what is warm can produce only warmth; but the science of medicine can be employed to produce either disease or health."[19] Heidegger returns to this topic in his lectures on Plato's "Sophist" (discussed below) and in his 1931 lectures on *Metaphysics* Θ 1–3, where he discusses beings "without souls" and those that are "besouled." He draws a strong contrast between the way in which besouled beings essentially possess a soul and the way in which they might inessentially possess a motorcycle (!). However, he focuses on the difference between "δυνάμεις ἄλογοι and δυνάμεις μετὰ λόγον—that is, forces without discourse ["reason" in the above quotation from Aristotle] and forces directed by discourse [reason]" (Heidegger 1995, 99–100; my interpolation).

Heidegger argues that λόγος does not mean reason: "The Aristotelian problem makes sense only if λόγος has a certain kinship to αἴσθησις [perception]" based on the fact that both "in some way uncover and unconceal that toward which they are directed" and, hence, are both "connected with ἀληθεύειν [truth as *alethēia*]" (Heidegger 1995, 107; my interpolations). Thus, Heidegger argues that, for Aristotle, humans are "the living being who lives in such a way that his life, as a way to be, is defined in an originary way by the command of language." We uncover truth in seeing, but also in naming what we see and drawing it into our sociolinguistic world—much as Léon Foucault "saw" the rotation of Earth and created a symbolic (albeit nonlinguistic) way to display it to others with his pendulum.

Living beings besides Dasein perceive and appear to make choices; they have what Edelman calls "primary consciousness." Heidegger admits that for Aristotle, the category of those without λόγος may overlap the category of the ensouled. He notes that Aristotle does not always articulate the distinction between a being that can do or not do something (i.e., besouled, animate things) and a being that can do or do the opposite thing (i.e., beings μετὰ λόγον). A cat can choose to eat or not eat, but it cannot choose to consume fewer calories to lose weight. It is the kind of consciousness capable of the second choice that is crucial to Heidegger's thought (and arguably Aristotle's thought as well).[20] In his 1922 text, Heidegger discusses science as an intellectual virtue, noting its subordination to wisdom and the corresponding subordination of human concerns to "beings that always are," and says,—"σοφία [wisdom] does not in any sense have human life as its intentional toward-which" (Heidegger 2002c, 136–37; my interpolation). In terms of this view, the natural world, humans, and animals are not the primary concerns of σοφία and, hence, of philosophy.

This leads, at the end of this text, to a premonition of Heidegger's critique of modernity. "What becomes clear on the basis of these interpretations is the extent to which a particular ontology of a particular domain of being [the human] and the logic of a particular kind of addressing [science] came to be regarded, in consequence of the inclination toward falling found in interpreting, as *the one and true ontology* and *the one and true* logic, and as such came to dominate in a decisive manner not only the history of ontology and logic but also that of spirit itself, i.e., the history of human existence." In short, the post-Aristotelian and, specifically, Christian history of philosophy ignores Being in favor of beings, and values science (or scientism) above "real" philosophy. In another echo of *Toward a Definition of Philosophy*, Heidegger states that this tradition misreads Aristotle because, "The origin of the 'categories' does not lie in λόγος as such. Nor are these 'categories' read off from 'things.' Rather, they are the basic modes of a particular kind of addressing of a particular domain of objects...and consist of those objects of dealing one can be concerned with and directed to in terms of routine tasks." This misreading, he goes on to argue, is deeply connected to the shift from Greek to Latin, symbolized for Heidegger by the shift from φύσις to nature, as discussed in chapter 1: "The 'objectivity' of the theoretical definition of objects in the sense of 'nature,' an 'objectivity' that in turn first grew out of this starting point for epistemology, then took the lead regarding the problem of the sense of being" (Heidegger 2002c, 144–45; his emphasis, my interpolations). That is, traditional philosophy is fundamentally flawed; it is a dualistic metaphysics developed to answer the epistemological problems crystallized by Descartes. Aristotle's project was, by contrast, the same one that Heidegger later undertook—an attempt to do fundamental ontology accompanied by a correspondingly different understanding of our relation to the world.

Notes

1. See the discussion of ψυχή in chapter 1 for Heidegger's use of "psychic" here.

2. See, for instance, Theodore Kisiel's invaluable *The Genesis of Heidegger's Being and Time*, p. 40 and elsewhere.

3. On this, and with specific regard to *Toward a Definition of Philosophy*, see Jeffrey Andrew Barash's contribution to Kisiel and van Buren's collection on the early Heidegger, "Heidegger's Ontological 'Destruction' of Western Intellectual Traditions" (Kisiel and van Buren 1994, 111–21, especially page 112). It is hard to imagine Heidegger's teaching having the profound effect that Barash's sources describe if he only recapitulated the usual view of intentionality, etc.

4. Compare the quotation from Dreyfus in chapter 2: "It is only because our interests are *not* objects in our experience that they can play this fundamental role of organizing our experience into meaningful patterns or regions" (Dreyfus 1979, 274; his emphasis).

5. Heidegger says later, in "Modern Science, Metaphysics, and Mathematics" (1936), that "there are no mere facts, but...a fact is only what it is in the light of the fundamental conception" (Heidegger 1993, 272). His thought here has obvious connections to John Dewey's concept of the "reflex arc" (Thayer 1970, 262–74) and to the work of Maurice Merleau-Ponty.

6. Compare "The *world worlds*" in "The Origin of the Work of Art" (Heidegger 1993, 170; his emphasis).

7. I owe this point to Barash's "Heidegger's Ontological 'Destruction' of Western Intellectual Traditions" (Kisiel and van Buren 1994, 119), though the context of his discussion is quite different.

8. Note the very early reference to *Ereignis*. For a much more detailed discussion of the relationship between *Ereignis* (the event) and *er-eignen* (to appropriate) in the later Heidegger, see my *The Madwoman's Reason: The Concept of the Appropriate in Ethical Thought* (1998).

9. George Kovacs, "Philosophy as Primordial Science in Heidegger's Courses of 1919" (Kisiel and van Buren 1993, 91–107; quotations are from page 95).

10. Cf. Hubert L. Dreyfus's similar discussion of *Being and Time* in *Being-in-the-World* (Dreyfus 1991, 112–27).

11. Heidegger speaks approvingly enough here of Lask's work that I felt licensed to apply one of his comments to Heidegger himself in the epigraph to this chapter (see Heidegger 2008, 69).

12. Cf., for example, "The opinion which is fated to be ultimately agreed to by all who investigate, is what we mean by truth, and the object represented by this opinion is the real" (Peirce 1955, 38).

13. Note that "indebted" (*verschuldet*) and "debt" (*Schuld*) in the above quotation are closely related to guilt (also *Schuld*) and hence to the concept of fallenness in *Being and Time*.

14. In his contribution to *Reading Heidegger from the Start*, "The Place of Aristotle in the Development of Heidegger's Phenomenology," Walter Brogan also comments on the ways in which *Phenomenological Interpretations of Aristotle* presages *Being and Time* (Kisiel and van Buren 1994, 213–27, especially pages 213–16); David Farrell Krell makes a similar comment in the same volume (Kisiel and van Buren 1994, 365).

15. Compare "What is Metaphysics?" (1929).

16. David Farrell Krell's contribution to *Reading Heidegger from the Start* (Kisiel and van Buren 1994, 361–79) focuses on the concept of "life," rather than the mind/body problem, but offers a similar reading. He points out that the word "ruinance" itself is "nothing, *das Nichts*." He also draws a line similar to the one we will follow from here through *Logic: The Question of Truth* and "What is Metaphysics?" Krell says that this line "would not circumvent *Being and Time* but pierce it through at *one* point—the point at which…the very being of Dasein is defined as nullity" (Kisiel and van Buren 1994, 378, my emphasis). For more on this, see chapter 4.

17. Ayer: "in all sentences of the form 'p is true,' the phrase 'is true' is logically superfluous" (Ayer 1952, 88).

18. Compare the discussion of Dreyfus's comment about rules in Wittgenstein in chapter 2.

19. *Metaphysics*, Theta 2, 1046a,b. I take this text to be later than the *Nicomachean Ethics* (though the same may not be true for all of the *Metaphysics*) because of the references to the *Ethics*. For Heidegger's view of the chronology here, see *Plato's Sophist* (Heidegger 1997, 45).

20. We will return to the question of nonhuman consciousness, especially with reference to Derrida's critique of Heidegger on this point, in chapter 8.

4 Truth, Being, and Mind

Only what can speak can be silent.

—Martin Heidegger (*Plato's Sophist*, 1997)

I: *Plato's Sophist*

Heidegger's abiding interest in Aristotle is perhaps best evidenced by the fact that more pages of his 1924–25 lectures on the "Sophist" are devoted to the *Nicomachean Ethics* and the *Metaphysics* than to Plato's dialogue (a rather masterful feat of Socratic/Platonic indirection). These lectures fall in the chronological gap between the 1922 introduction to the proposed book on Aristotle and *Being and Time* in 1927, but they are in many ways continuous with the lectures on the ancient Greeks that are generally considered to belong to the "later Heidegger." They also provide a clear illustration of how Heidegger's thinking about consciousness evolves. Furthermore, these lectures in conjunction with the later ones on Parmenides allow us to see why Heidegger considered his philosophy to be a natural outgrowth of the ancient Greeks' philosophies. They also suggest why he pursued the two paths he did after the so-called *Kehre*. These paths were a positive account he believes traces back to Aristotle and the pre-Socratic thinkers and a correlative negative account of the technological age that developed as a result of Roman/Christian appropriation, not to say corruption, of that tradition. ("Christianity is basically responsible for this phenomenon of the decline of philosophy," he tells us in the lectures on "Sophist" [Heidegger 1997, 176].)

These lectures are also linked to his concern with nothingness and not being, which appear earlier but come to the forefront in the *Kehre*, because "The Sophist" focuses in part on what it means to say something is or is not. The Stranger tells Theaetetus, "you yourself must clarify for us what you properly mean when you utter this word ὄν" (244a), and Heidegger comments in his lectures, *"That is the genuinely central concern of this passage and of the whole dialogue."* He gives two "reasons" why "the forgetting of this question [of the meaning of the ὄν] is easy for us today": (1) everyone already knows the meaning of "Being" and (2) the word "Being" is so abstract it cannot be defined at all (Heidegger 1997, 309; cf. Heidegger 2000, 42). A few pages later, Heidegger argues that for the ancient Greeks, "The meaning of Being implicitly guiding this ontology is Being = presence" (Heidegger 1997, 323). What exists for the ancient Greeks is what is present to them—that is, what comes to them from physis. Note the implicit contrast here between this kind of presence and the present-at-hand in the modern world. The presence of things is a given to the ancient Greeks; things are encountered by them as already meaningful. The presence of things is rarely, if ever, the bare, abstract contemplation of decontextualized sensory perception characteristic of the present-at-hand.

Heidegger already linked Being and presence earlier in the "Sophist" lectures: "ὄν, the Being of beings itself, is primarily interpreted as presence" (Heidegger 1997, 155). In the Appendix to that page, he also states that, for the ancient Greeks, "the *Being of beings is interpreted (on the basis of) time*." Why? Because "the letting be encountered is based, in its possibilities, on the Being of Dasein. But the Being of Dasein is temporality. And the pure letting the world be encountered is a making present. *As such*, it is only temporally that it can express *itself* in the appropriate speaking about the world." For Aristotle and the other Greeks, "What is present is genuine Being, and the Being *no longer* of the past, as well as the Being not yet can be determined on the basis of it ..." (Heidegger 1997, 439–40; his emphasis, final ellipsis due to illegibility of the handwritten source text). In other words, the Greeks understand the past and the future out of what is present to them in the present moment, out of what *is* for them right now. This is how they interpret the fact that if things exist, they must exist for some consciousness that brings them into temporal order. Tables do not exist for chairs, but they do exist for, say, cats and humans. Their existence for cats, however, is not existence *as* tables and chairs, since the cat does not think of them as such. For things to exist as the beings they are, they must exist for entities that have what Edelman calls "second order consciousness"—that is, for Dasein. And Dasein, as Heidegger notes, is temporal to its core. Our knowledge is dependent on how we exist in the world, and time is not a part of the world outside of our experience, but a reflection of the nature of our experience.

These concepts should all be familiar by now, as should the link between this line of thought and Heidegger's critique of technology, which assumes the "reality" of time. However, these lectures also reveal how Heidegger's account of Dasein's existence as consciousness draws from his reading of the ancient Greeks. Thus, a deep internal link is demonstrated between the two main realms of thought—modernity and the ancient Greeks—in Heidegger's later work. He explains his preoccupation with ancient Greek texts in *Plato's Sophist* by stating, "Precisely in what we no longer see, in what has become an everyday matter, something is at work that was once the object of the greatest spiritual exertions ever undertaken in Western history" (PS 7). He also declares, "Unconcealedness is a determination of beings—insofar as they are encountered." Disclosure as alētheia "is itself a mode of Being, and indeed not of the beings which are first disclosed—those of the world—but instead of the beings we call human Dasein" (Heidegger 1997, 11–12). Dasein reveals itself as the being that dis-covers truths, discloses a world of entities that would simply be undifferentiated "stuff" unless we encountered them. A few pages later, he attributes this view to Aristotle, whom he quotes as saying, "ἀληθεύει ἡ ψυχή" (Heidegger 1997, 16)—the soul speaks the truth. This is because, as we saw earlier, "what is ἀληθές is the πρᾶγμα; ἀληθεύειν is a determination of the Being of life"—that is, what is unconcealed truth arises in response to the questions we as ensouled, or conscious, beings ask in the course of our everyday, practical lives (Heidegger 1997, 19).

Heidegger returns to the topic of the soul later in these lectures in conjunction with the final determination of the Sophists' technē. He does so in terms similar to those discussed in the previous chapter with regard to Aristotle and the *Nicomachean Ethics*. Aristotle (and Plato) begin the discussion of cleansing the soul by making the distinction between "the body of what is without a soul" and "the body of what is alive." The latter, Heidegger tells us, is "given not only from the outside ... but to be given from the inside, as we say, i.e., given as a body for the living being whose body it is." From this idea he draws the two conclusions we have previously noted: "My relation to my body is therefore one that is specifically psychic, i.e., this relation includes the possibility of my being 'disposed' in relation to my body"; and bodies with a soul can be "purified" or cleansed not only externally, but also internally through gymnastics and the medical arts. The first point addresses the unspoken distinction between Dasein and other bodies with souls that are not "disposed" with regard to their bodies but simply live through them—that is, they lack secondary consciousness. The second point reminds us that, for Dasein, causes can produce opposite effects. A police officer can learn to wrestle a man down under certain conditions but not under others. By contrast, a dog can learn to take a man down on command, but once the command is given, the dog will not normally stop even if circumstances change. If the man abuses his skill, he must be educated or cleansed internally. The dog, however, must be retrained through external action (Heidegger 1997, 250).

In Dasein, both the "correct" behavior and its "deformation" are possible because of the nature of the human psyché. Both behaviors depend on two facts: Dasein's "soul" or form is already in motion (as opposed to, for example, the form of a stone); and Dasein's soul has some sense of what it is on the way to. It is not merely moving toward its goal but striving toward it. In the negative case this motion has "gone awry." A dog that attacks a man has not "gone awry," because it is following either its instincts or its training; it has done what it was meant to do. A person who wrestles another to the ground in a malicious attack, on the other hand, has deviated from what Dasein was meant to be. The soul's "being-underway," according to Heidegger, reflects Dasein's ontological structure as Being-in. Here, he emphasizes that this Being-in is "permeated by ἄγνοια," which he defines as "a certain infatuation with immediately given appearances, on the basis of which all further experiences of the world are interpreted, interrogated, and explained." This point echoes a common theme: "The knowledge arising in this way can become science and as such can be nurtured and cherished," though it also contains a striving "toward an ἀληθεύειν which has the potential to break through the actual ignorance" (Heidegger 1997, 253–56).

This passage can be glossed two ways. The more "normal" way would be to take the case of someone like a trained wrestler, who may think that he sees a world in which he can attack people from behind and rob them with impunity. He may even make a "science" of such attacks and become quite skillful at them. But his soul, or his form, will always be the form of a Dasein capable of seeing the world as one in which money is less important than living ethically. This phenomenon may manifest itself as guilt, remorse, or deep dissatisfaction with life. No matter what his circumstances, part of the wrestler will strive toward what Plato would consider a healthier, less deformed way of life based on a truer perception of the world and his place in it.

But Heidegger leaves open another way of interpreting this passage. On a societal level, an interpretation of the world based on "idle talk" (a term that appears several times in these lectures) might see a life of leisure as the most desirable life, no matter how it is attained. This desire might lead to a science geared toward reducing labor and producing more items with less expenditure of energy. Such a science, based on efficiencies of scale, might emphasize the 'benefit' of reducing everything to potential energy, or what Heidegger called "standing reserve" a decade later. We will see where this line of thought eventually takes Heidegger, but my point here is to emphasize the close connection between the problems of modernity, his interpretation of the ancient Greek texts, and his views on the nature of "consciousness"—that is, Dasein.

Psyché is increasingly thematized in these lectures, always in terms compatible, and on occasion identical, with our earlier account. In interpreting the passage on the changing and unchanging in "Sophist," Heidegger writes, "The soul is the being in which we can see that in fact στάσις is co-present with movement. The soul is movement is the sense of ὄρεξις, and, as Plato shows in the *Symposium*, the soul does not merely have desire as one among many other lived experiences, but instead the soul is desire and nothing else" (Heidegger 1997, 382).[1] This ongoing desire or emptiness of the "soul" resonates with our previous discussion of "ruinance," but here the desire to know is secondary to the letting-be-known of beings.[2] "Only if there is a possible conjunction of what is properly visible in beings, only if beings themselves allow something like a disclosure of themselves in the character of the 'as,' is there a λέγειν; and only if there is a λέγειν is human existence possible" (Heidegger 1997, 399–400). "Λέγειν" clearly means much more here than the capacity for speech. It is the core of the "as structure" that allows Dasein to see things as the things they are—that is, it allows us to categorize and name things in ways that facilitate our interactions with them and with each other.[3]

This last point is key, because caring, Being-in-the-World, and Being-with are essential features of Dasein's existence: "Already, in its very first aspect, λέγειν is understood as utterance and is genuinely and primarily understood as a speaking with others *about something*. The phonetic character is not apprehended as noise—that is a purely theoretical construct" (Heidegger 1997, 404; his emphasis). The lectures end, however, with an admonition that underscores the difficulty of using modern terms such as "consciousness" in engaging with Heidegger's analyses. "The identification of the ψυχή with consciousness and of consciousness with subjectivity injects into the interpretation of Plato's philosophy an ungodly confusion from which we will never extricate ourselves as long as we have not learned to disregard the worn-out categories of modern logic" (Heidegger 1997, 421).

II: *Logic: The Question of Truth*

Heidegger's 1925–26 lectures published under the title, *Logic: The Question of Truth*, are as much about logic in the usual sense as *Philosophical Interpretations of Aristotle* is about Aristotle or as *Plato's Sophist* is about Plato's "Sophist." Instead, these lectures include at least three other discussions that are central to Heidegger's thought: a careful delineation of the similarities and differences between his thought and Husserl's; a fascinating reading of Kant's account(s) of time in *The Critique of Pure Reason*; and, correlative with both, a relatively clear explanation of what Heidegger understands by "mind" in relationship to "body." The lectures also contain a discussion of "care" and an interesting version of the speech act theory hinted at in *Toward a Definition of Philosophy* (Heidegger 2010, 109–10, 121, and elsewhere; cf. Heidegger 2008, 89). As is the case with much of the early work, however, this text has traditionally been read as a precursor to *Being and Time*, which was written the following summer, rather than as an important step in the development of Heidegger's thought in its own right.[4] To the extent that *Logic* is a precursor, it deserves attention for discussing some of the same ideas—for example, care and the temporality of Dasein—as *Being and Time* but without much of the specialized vocabulary. To the extent that *Logic* explicitly engages with some of the key issues here, it is worth a careful reading on its own account. Given the limits of space, I will focus this section primarily on how Heidegger defines "mind" and "body" and the relationship between the two in the text, which was written before his thought became wrapped in the existential perspective and more obscure language of *Being and Time*.

I say "more obscure language" because the language in these earlier lectures is unusually direct, especially with regard to the differences between Heidegger's thought and Husserl's. Describing the problem of consciousness, Heidegger states the following:

> Basically, we are in a situation where we have to see these two separate orders or fields or spheres or regions as coming together in unity: that which has being and that which has validity, the sensible and the non-sensible, the real and the ideal, the historical and the transhistorical. We have not yet apprehended an original kind of being in terms of which we could understand these two fields as possible and as belonging to that of being. Philosophers don't even ask about such being.[5]

He goes on to note. "Husserl has not asked the question. Rather, within the framework of psychologism and in a manner that derives from psychologism, he asks what the mental as such must be if it is able to as the real in relation to the ideal" (Heidegger 2010, 77). These lectures also emphasize "non-thematic absorption" as our primary way of relating to things in the world. Dreyfus regards this idea, as expressed in *Being and Time*, as a key move beyond Husserlian intentionality, though he notes that it is not clearly argued in that later text (Dreyfus 1991, 69–70). Here it is (somewhat) more directly explained:

> Although our knowledge remains (within certain limits) constantly related to its firsthand lived world, we mostly do not have things present 'bodily' …, not even—and especially not—when we are involved with those things. In the precise moment that I write on the chalkboard something I am saying, I certainly do sense the resistance of the board, and the board is bodily given to me. However, in a strict sense, the board is not bodily present to me as I write. Rather, I am present to the words I am writing and their meaning.

By contrast, Husserl relies on intuition defined in terms of "bodily presence," which Heidegger argues "is geared to theoretical apprehension and knowledge" (Heidegger 2010, 85–86).

The problem of consciousness understood as a non-sensible "inside" that stands in an external relationship to a sensible "outside" reappears throughout this text. With regard to the mind as "inside," Heidegger asks, again with uncharacteristic directness, "Are these [mental] phenomena … actually inside us in the way that the circulation of the blood and the function of gastric juices are, with the simple difference that they are not sensible and cannot be treated in a direct chemical and physical way? Or does what we mean by thinking, judging, and so forth—this 'mental' as such—have its own structure and its own kind of being?" The answer to this question, he acknowledges, requires recognizing the importance of the concept of intentionality. "Thinking is the thinking-of-what-is-thought, because thinking, as mental, already necessarily has the structure of self-directedness-to-something.... It is not first of all something real only, as it were, within consciousness, and then afterwards, by some kind of mechanism, related to something outside." My thought of a particular chair is not extrinsically related to the chair, but is instead precisely a thought-of-that-chair. To borrow a case from Wittgenstein, my expecting Paul to tea is an expecting-Paul. Heidegger says "the mental is first and only this very self-directedness and as such is it 'real'." In other words, consciousness simply is its intentionality (Heidegger 2010, 78–80). Moreover, this is what makes truth possible. My ideas, beliefs, or expectations are "proven" true or false by the chair or by Paul's arrival.[6] At least provisionally, "Truth is the identity of the meant and the intuited" (Heidegger 2010, 89).

Many of the ways in which these lectures presage *Being and Time* carry forward this view of existence (i.e., Dasein) in terms of its directedness-outward. "Existence is, in itself and by its very nature, world-open, open for the world; and corresponding to that, the world is dis-closed, opened-up. The primary form of that disclosedness [cf. truth as alētheia] is the opening up of whatever thing is being questioned." The "truth" of things consists of the disclosures or uncovering of them as the objects of our questioning comportment, just as the "truth" of my thought-of-the-chair is "proven" by the chair. Furthermore, "the thing we encounter is uncovered in terms of the end-for-which of its serviceability. It is already posited in meaning—it already makes sense." My thought-of-the-chair primarily views the chair in a context of "for-sitting" and only secondarily as the abstract object of my thought-of-the-chair or as a philosophical example or a potential piece of firewood in a blizzard. Heidegger warns that we must not "understand this to mean that we were first given a something that is free of meaning, and then a meaning gets attached to it. Rather, what is first of all 'given' ... [is] the 'for-sitting'." Consciousness is this open directedness toward the world, but it is always already immersed in a world of meanings (Heidegger 2010, 121; my interpolations). "More precisely," he continues, "as existing [i.e., as Dasein] ... I am an act of intelligently dealing-with" (Heidegger 2010, 123; my interpolation).

This, again, is tied to truth—specifically in the context of Aristotle, for whom *legein*, or speaking, is, according to Heidegger, "the showing of a being." As we just saw with regard to intentionality, "to indicate a being is to be already present with that being, even when the subject matter that the speech indicates is not bodily present but only intended. Even when absent, the very sense of the statement entails that the being itself is intended, not some representation or image that 'corresponds' to the absent being." When I stand with my back to a chair, I may verbally refer to it or I may back up and sit in it without looking. In both cases, the object of my "speech act" and of my intending-to-sit is the chair as "for-sitting." This internal relationship between the mental state and the chair means that "truth is not a relation that is 'just there' between two beings that themselves are 'just there'—one mental, the other physical" as in the traditional view. Rather, "it is the relation of existence [Dasein] as such to its very world. It is the world-openness of existence that is itself uncovered—existence whose very being unto the world gets disclosed/uncovers in and with its being unto the world" (Heidegger 2010, 137; my interpolation). That is, the truths I might speak about the chair as a philosophical example also disclose the truth of my existence as someone concerned about chairs (or philosophy). Thus, in this text, we see the empty outward movement that is the essential nature of consciousness. In *Being and Time*, by contrast, it is not the structural emptiness of Dasein that comes to the fore, but rather the lived, psychological emptiness of *Angst*.

III: *Being and Time*

A Short Detour Through History

Being and Time is Heidegger's best-known book, but my argument requires a rethinking of how that incomplete work fits into the development of his thought. While it clearly picks up on themes from the earlier works we have looked at, it does so from a perspective that moves away from the preoccupation of those texts with science, modernity, and ancient Greek philosophy. It also moves away from the limits of the contemporary, scientific-technological understanding of human nature and humans' place in the world, including the legacy of Cartesian dualism. Instead, *Being and Time* focuses on a more temporally undifferentiated, not to say universalized, concept of the root causes of human *Angst*.

I will offer two main reasons for giving relatively short shrift to what is often considered to be Heidegger's *magnum opus*, beyond the sheer impossibility of offering a full reading of it in the space available here. These reasons are derived from the biographical background of the publication of *Being and Time* provided in Theodore Kisiel's *The Genesis of Heidegger's Being and Time*; and from Heidegger's own later comments about why he never completed the work. Although some of the existential themes from *Being and Time* are still apparent in his later work from the early 1930s—considered in the next chapter of the present book—they are presented in that later work in a context that focuses not on human existence, but on wider ontological questions.

According to Kisiel, the most important steps in the historical saga of *Being and Time* begin in August 1925 (the summer before the lectures on "Logic"), when Heidegger's name was put forward for a full professorship at Marburg. The nomination received a negative response in January 1926 due to his limited "literary accomplishments." Heidegger reports that in the following month, the dean of the philosophy faculty at Marburg told him, "Professor Heidegger, you have got to publish something now," adding, "But it must be printed quickly." Heidegger chose to publish the "long-guarded" manuscript of *Being and Time*. In May 1926, he wrote to Karl Jaspers that "it is for me a transition work," a move away from traditional phenomenology because Husserl apparently found "the whole thing strange." Heidegger took his mentor's reaction to mean that he had "already de facto" progressed further along that path than he had realized. In June 1926, the Marburg faculty again put Heidegger's name forward, based on the impending publication of the book, but the request was denied the following November. At the end of that year, after conversations with Jaspers, Heidegger decided to delay the publication of part 3 of division 1. This decision was made, he reported later, on the day the two philosophers learned of Rainer Maria Rilke's death. He also later reported thinking at the time that "in the course of the year everything could be said more clearly. That was a delusion."

The book as it now exists was published in late April 1927. In 1975, Heidegger identified *The Basic Problems of Phenomenology* (1927) as the revised part 3 of division 1 (but see the discussion of this below). Division 2 was most likely abandoned in 1929–30, leaving division 1, parts 1 and 2 as what Kisiel calls "a permanent fragment." Nevertheless, as Heidegger told Rudolph Bultmann in October 1927, he had "proved that I can get something into print" (Kisiel 1995, 479–89).

Heidegger never offers a direct explanation of why he didn't finish division 2 of *Being and Time*, but his later works provide some clues relevant to our discussion. In the Addendum to his lectures on Parmenides (1942–43) he emphasizes that Dasein is not to be understood as a plurality of subjectivities or selves: "Modern man has a 'lived experience' of the world and thinks the world in those terms, i.e., in terms of himself as the being that, as ground, lies at the foundation of all explanation and ordering of beings as a whole." With obvious reference to the work of Martin Buber, he adds that replacing the self with an I-Thou relation or with "the community, the nation, the people, the continent, and the planet, these in no way, metaphysically speaking, cancels out the subjectivity of modern man" (Heidegger 1992, 165). Similarly, the "Note" added to "On the Essence of Truth" in 1949 says that

the thinking attempted in the lecture comes to fulfillment in the essential experience that a nearness to the truth of Being is first prepared for historical man on the basis of the Da-sein into which man can enter. Every kind of anthropology and all subjectivity of man as a subject is not merely left behind—as it was already in *Being and Time*—and the truth of Being sought as the ground of a transformed historical position; rather, the movement of the lecture is such that it sets out to think from this other ground (Dasein). The course of the questioning is intrinsically the way of a thinking which, instead of furnishing representations and concepts, experiences and tests itself as a transformation of its relatedness to Being (Heidegger 1993, 138).

This passage suggests that Heidegger thought *Being and Time* remained too close to the logic of subject and object, which created the possibility of the kind of misinterpretations of his ideas found in the work of Jean-Paul Sartre, as suggested by the reference to the "Letter on Humanism" (1947).

The "Letter on Humanism" itself is a key text for understanding Heidegger's attitude toward his unfinished earlier project. There, he notes the shift from the focus on human Dasein (a term aligned with the traditional thinking he labeled "metaphysics") to the focus on Being: "Metaphysics closes itself to the simple essential fact that man essentially occurs only in his essence, where he is claimed by Being" (Heidegger 1993, 227). He rejects the theory that *Being and Time* "ended in a dead alley," because "the thinking that hazards a few steps in *Being and Time* has even today not advanced beyond that publication." He adds that "perhaps in the meantime it has in one respect come farther into its own matter." Part of the problem, he seems to indicate, is the unwillingness of his readers to do the hard work needed to follow his thought. "Whether the realm of the truth of Being is a blind alley, or whether it is the free space in which freedom conserves its essence is something each one may judge after he himself has tried to go the designated way, or even better, after he has gone a better way, that is, a way befitting the question" (Heidegger 1993, 246–47). He acknowledges, however, that terms such as "fundamental ontology" in *Being and Time* "were bound to lead immediately and inevitably into error. For the terms and the conceptual language corresponding to them were not rethought by readers from that matter particularly to be thought; rather, the matter was conceived according to the established terminology in its customary meaning" (Heidegger 1993, 259).

In implicit contrast to Sartre and the other existentialists, Heidegger notes, "For us, 'world' does not at all signify beings or any realm of beings but the openness of Being.... Man is never first and foremost man on the hither side of the world, as a 'subject,' whether this is taken as 'I' or "We.' Nor is he ever simply a mere subject which always simultaneously is related to objects, so that his essence lies in the subject-object relation" (Heidegger 1993, 252). While *Being and Time* may not be wrong about philosophical issues such as the mind/body problem, this comment suggests that the book can at least be misleading in important ways.

Fifteen years later, Heidegger is more forthright. In describing the shift from an emphasis on Being to one on *Ereignis* in "Time and Being" (1962), he states, "The attempt in *Being and Time* ... to derive human spatiality from temporality is untenable" (Heidegger 1972, 23). In the related seminar, he added, "Already in *Being and Time*, time is thought in its relation to *alētheia*," but he notes a few lines earlier that "this is not explicitly named in the part of *Being and Time* that was published" (Heidegger 1972, 28–29). In the *Four Seminars* (1966–73), Heidegger again discusses Sartre's reading of *Being and Time* in the context of the "meaning of being," where "'meaning' is to be understood from 'project,' which is to be explained by 'understanding.'"[7] The problem is the possibility of taking "project" as "a structure of subjectivity—which is how Sartre takes it, by basing himself on Descartes." For Heidegger, the meaning of Being is determined not by Dasein but by Being itself. For this reason, he says, his later work "replaced the expression 'meaning of being' with the 'truth of being'" (Heidegger 2003, 40–41). Because the "truth of being" becomes the focus of the texts in which Heidegger most fully develops the argument under discussion here, I will follow David Farrell Krell in tracing a different path through Heidegger's work. My path is not identical to Krell's, but like his "would not circumvent *Being and Time* but pierce it through at *one* point—the point at which ... the very being of Dasein is defined as nullity" (Kisiel and van Buren 1994, 378; my emphasis).

Mind, Consciousness, Dasein

Despite the general truth of what I said above, the second section of division 1 of *Being and Time* returns to Heidegger's earlier preoccupation with "How the Analytic of Dasein is to be Distinguished from Anthropology, Psychology, and Biology." The structure of these scientific disciplines "needs to be attacked in new ways which must have their source in ontological problematic," because the Cartesian subject at the center of modern science relies on an uninvestigated concept of the *sum* of "*cogito ergo sum*" (Heidegger 1962, 71). Dasein in contrast, is not such a subject, but an empty openness to the world in which it finds itself—an openness that it already encounters as intersubjective and meaningful. His use of the word "Dasein" was intended, Heidegger tells us twenty years later, "to characterize with a *single* term both the relation of Being to the essence of man and the essential relation of man to the openness ('there' ['*Da*']) of Being [*Sein*] as such." At the same time, he insists we must not think "the term 'Dasein' is used in place of 'consciousness'" (Heidegger 1998, 283; his emphasis, translator's interpolations).

In *Being and Time*, he notes that for the biological and social sciences, "Dasein is tacitly conceived in advance as something present-at-hand.... Yet presence-at-hand is the kind of Being which belongs to entities whose character is not that of Dasein" (Heidegger 1962, 150).[8] He states several times, "Dasein is in each case mine," but he adds, "what if this should be the very reason why, proximally and for the most part, Dasein *is not itself*?" He gives two reasons for this not-being-itself: the reason Dreyfus gives in *Being-in-the-World*—"we have shown that a bare subject without a world never 'is' proximally, nor is it ever given"; and the reason seized on by Sartre—"Dasein's 'Essence' is grounded in its existence." These two ideas are combined in Heidegger: "If in each case Dasein is its Self only in *existing*, then the constancy of the Self no less than the possibility of its 'failure to stand by itself' requires that we formulate the question existentially and ontologically," but "man's *'substance'* is not spirit as a synthesis of soul and body; it is rather *existence*" (Heidegger 1962, 151–53; his emphasis).[9]

This existence lies before and beyond the subject/object, the inner/outer divide that comes to us from the Cartesian tradition. In *What Computers Can't Do*, Dreyfus considers the objection that Heidegger's emphasis on our pragmatic actions in the world (filled with equipment and socially defined tasks to be carried out for the sake of others) ignores the reality of the "inner" life of the Cartesian subject. Dreyfus responds by invoking the way in which Heidegger's work goes behind or beyond the subject/object distinction on which this complaint rests:

> This seems plausible only because one is still confusing this human world with some sort of physical universe. My personal plans and my memories are inscribed in the things around me just as are the public goals of men in general. My memories are stored in the familiar look of a chair.... My plans and fears are already built into my experience of some objects as attractive and other as to be avoided. (Dreyfus 1979, 266).

To take another example, a major remodeling by the new owners of my family's former home makes it no longer the house I grew up in because I can no longer find my childhood memories there. The house I grew up in now exists only in my mind, in my brother's mind, and in old photographs. But my memories "are stored," Dreyfus argues, in those photos and in my conversations with my brother as much as in my mind.

Heidegger makes a similar argument against the view that a "perceptive retention of an assertion about something" can be seen "as a 'procedure' by which a subject provides itself with representations of something which remain stored up 'inside' as having thus been appropriated, and with regard to which the question of how they 'agree' with actuality can occasionally arise." The truth of my memories is not verified as much by whether the memories agree with an "actuality" that no longer exists (and which can only partially be represented by photos) as it is through conversations with people whose memories overlap, but cannot coincide, with my own. However, the point of those conversations will rarely be to verify the memories, but rather to make a disappeared place available to all of us involved in the conversation as part of our current being-with each other.

Heidegger describes this "process" by saying, "When Dasein directs itself towards something and grasps it, it does not somehow first get out of an inner sphere in which it has been proximally encapsulated, but its primary kind of Being is such that it is always 'outside' alongside entities which it encounters and which belong to a world already discovered." In the case of my memories, I seek out "verification" of where the piano sat in my childhood home because I am already in some sense "out there" in the past with it. If I was not out there, the questions would not arise. "Nor is any inner sphere abandoned when Dasein dwells alongside the entity to be known, and determines its character; but even in this 'being-outside alongside the object, Dasein is still 'inside', if we understand this in the correct sense; that is to say, it is itself 'inside' as a Being-in-the-world which knows." In other words, what "I" am in the moment the question arises is precisely the being for whom that is a question and for whom it has some importance. Here again, we see how the question of truth is interwoven with the nature of "mind" (i.e., the "problem of consciousness" understood in terms of a relationship between the "inner" and the "outer") in Heidegger's text.

This last passage leads to one of Heidegger's clearest statements about the relationship between "inside" and "outside": "And furthermore, the perceiving of what is known is not a process of returning with one's booty to the 'cabinet' of consciousness after one has gone out and grasped it; even in perceiving, retaining, and preserving, the Dasein which knows *remains outside*, and it does so *as Dasein*" (Heidegger 1962, 89; his emphasis). In pursuing truth or knowledge—whether the knowledge in question is how to fix an unready-to-hand pen that is out of ink or to fill in a childhood memory I cannot recreate—I am always already out there in the world, and it is out there where I will find the answers to the tacit or explicit questions I ask (though, in the case of memory, the answer may be "not available at this time"). I am never complete and closed off in myself. First, I am not simply myself as long as I live as embodied in a sociolinguistic world, which makes possible my existence as what I am. And secondly, I am not simply myself, because Dasein "is itself essentially *null*" (Heidegger 1962, 331; his emphasis); it is an empty openness.

Thus, we come belatedly to the existentialist side of *Being and Time*. I am this emptiness pushed forward in time by ruinance, always *unheimlich*, both eerie and without a home. My reaction to this truth, as we saw in the discussion of the earlier works, is to flee—to believe that back/out there somewhere, maybe in my past and now nonexistent home, I can find my essence, a meaning for my life, when what is my ownmost (*eigenst*) being-as-Dasein is to live authentically (*eigentlich*) in the empty openness of ex-sistence. Unlike beings whose nature is not that of Dasein, I can do or not do, be or not be what I am, and I must leap into that void without the benefit of faith.

For Heidegger, as for Aristotle, this emptiness is also the source of my freedom. But, *contra* Sartre, it is a constrained freedom. In fact, it is doubly constrained. As Sartre himself reluctantly admits, it is constrained by both the physical parameters of the world and the social meanings available to me in the world in which I find myself. Ice fishing was not a thing Aristotle could or could not do, nor could he have an opinion on the morality of *in vitro* fertilization or the possibility of interstellar travel. He could not even wonder where the piano stood in his childhood home. Furthermore, his opinions on whether a man was brave or a coward were constrained by what he understood to be the final end of human existence.

Of the choices of actions and beliefs available in his world, not all of them were "good" choices or, more accurately, choices a good man would make.

By contrast, Heidegger notes that the "Cartesian analysis of the 'world'" has the consequence that values become "determinate characteristics which a Thing possesses and they would be *present-at-hand*" (Heidegger 1962, 132). That is, values must become measurable in some way, or they become merely "subjective" and, hence, outside the realm of reason. He explains this idea more fully a few years later in *Introduction to Metaphysics*: in the modern age, "because values stand opposed to the Being of beings, in the sense of facts, they themselves cannot *be*. So instead one says that they are valid.... But validity is still too reminiscent of validity for a subject" (Heidegger 2000, 212–13; his emphasis). For Heidegger, again *contra* Sartre, this loss of a sense of intrinsic value is part of the damage done by the technological age. This disagreement is part of Heidegger's ongoing criticism of Sartre's work, even though Heidegger himself cannot offer a clear ethical path, given the limits of the modern world.

And Everything Else (Times Two)

Unlike Dreyfus's *Being-in-the-World*, the present discussion is not meant to be an exhaustive reading of *Being and Time*, any more than this entire project is meant to be an exhaustive interpretation of all aspects of Heidegger's massive *corpus*. Rather than delve more deeply into *Being and Time*, I would like to call attention to a facet of the work that is, ironically, both a limitation and a resource.

The reader may have noticed a recurrent "two-ness" in my discussion so far: two major ways of reading *Being and Time*, Dreyfus's and Sartre's; two options for ensouled beings, to do or not to do, complicated in the second case by the two possibilities of not doing for a reason or simply not doing; Dasein's ability to be or not be itself; two reasons Dasein is never simply and completely itself; Dasein's freedom as doubly constrained by the choices available in its physical and social world and, for Aristotle, by what a "good" man would or would not do; and the continuing vocabulary of "inner" and "outer" even where Heidegger is most eager to deny this "inner" as a sort of "'cabinet' of consciousness" (Heidegger 1962, 89). The limitation imposed by these persistent "two's" is one presented by *Being and Time* as a whole. Much like the Bible, it opens itself not only to many interpretations but to contradictory ones. The book can be taken, for example, as a continuation of Husserl's thought, as grounded in Husserl's thought, as a new start that would bypass Husserl's thought, or as a repudiation of Husserl's thought. Such is the case with almost anything else one might want to say about the work, including Heidegger's views on the mind/body problem and other metaphysical dualisms. This is one of many reasons for not engaging more fully with this text here. There is a danger of becoming so bogged down in the details that one may lose sight of one's point or of why *Being and Time* was interesting and important in the first place.

Another intriguing fact about this list of dualisms is that they are often internally divided by other sets of two. For example, the pair do/do not is internally divided by the pair not do/not do for reasons. In other cases they are twisted in some way (e.g., Dasein can be/cannot be itself, but itself is a nullity) or they are weakened (though never erased) by the use of quotation marks. One could consider this as evidence that *Being and Time* is one of the prime examples of the complexity of Heidegger's thought, but it is also evidence of the extent to which he was still trapped in the language and conceptual schemas provided to him by the world in which *he* found *himself*.[10] He sees the need to avoid the divine 1–2–3–4–(10)–12 sequences that have always ruled ontotheology, which may explain the "epicycles" of two-within-two noted above. But he has no good options for avoiding such pairs as do/not do, be/not be, and inner/outer.

This problem is clearest in the alternative between authenticity and inauthenticity. Heidegger refers more than once to an "undifferentiated" third option, in which we are "free either for authenticity or for inauthenticity or for a mode in which neither of these has been differentiated" (Heidegger 1962, 275).[11] This alternative, however, is easily lost sight of—most relevantly in Sartre's re-interpretation of the concepts into the exhaustive dualism of "good" and "bad" faith. The impact of this tendency to attribute a more dualistic view to Heidegger is clear when Derrida argues in "*Ousia* and *Grammé*" that in *Being and Time*, "all the conceptual pairs of opposites which serve the destruction of ontology are ordered around one fundamental axis: that which separates the authentic from the inauthentic and, in the very last analysis, primordial from fallen temporality.... Now, is not the opposition of the *primordial* to the *derivative* still metaphysical?"

This leads to a final "two"—two interrelated reasons to question the importance of *Being and Time* in the development of Heidegger's thought that go beyond the previously mentioned reservation about its status. These questions do not arise regarding the development of his career or of the understanding of his thought, for which *Being and Time* may indeed be central, but regarding his thought itself. Beyond all that Heidegger says or does not say about why the work was never completed, the project of grounding fundamental ontology on the temporality of Dasein seems doubly doomed from a post-Heideggerian/Derridian point of view (though Derrida never puts it in precisely this way). This is because, first, the ability of a more primordial understanding of time to undo the history of metaphysics is thrown into serious question, as Heidegger was no doubt aware, by the homology (which cannot simply be dismissed as accidental) in German, English, French, and other languages, between the present moment and what is present in the sense of present-at-hand—that is, the understanding of Being as the being of beings that governs the modern age. Secondly, the necessary failure of the effort can be seen as a result of the lack of clarity about what time itself *is* that persists in *Being and Time*, as Derrida suggests in "Ousia and Grammé." Derrida raises the possibility that "the concept of time, in all its aspects, belongs to metaphysics, and it names the domination of presence." Derrida, however, notes that this questioning "remains within Heidegger's thought" (Derrida 1982, 63–64). It is in the development of that thought during the "*Kehre*" (another *double* turning, away from *Being and Time* and from Heidegger's involvement in the Nazi party) that we will pick up the trail of Heidegger's understanding of the problem of consciousness, at the point where it crosses or pierces (in Krell's metaphor) *Being and Time*—the nullity of Dasein.

Notes

1. Cf. the discussion of zombies in chapter 1.
2. Cf. the discussion of ruinance in Heidegger, *Phenomenological Interpretations of Aristotle* in chapter 3.
3. Cf. the discussion of Edelman in chapter 2.
4. This seems to be the perspective taken by, for example, the translator, Thomas Sheehan in his Foreword (Heidegger 2010, ix), and by Walter Brogan in "The Place of Aristotle in the Development of Heidegger's Phenomenology" (Kisiel and van Buren 1994, 227).
5. The translator of *Logic: The Question of Truth* uses "being" where I use "Being." I leave "being" in quotations, but capitalize it elsewhere to maintain consistency with the rest of the present text.
6. That is, ideas, beliefs, and propositions all have what John Searle calls mind-to world or word-to-world "direction of fit" (Searle, 1979, 3–5). Having written my dissertation on the relationship between Searle's version of speech act theory and Derrida's early work, it seems both strange and natural to come full circle back to it here.
7. The translators of *The Four Seminars* use "being" in places where I use "Being." See note 5.
8. This is one of several places in *Being and Time*, including the passage cited next, where I have reservations about the capitalization of Being in the Macquarrie and Robinson translation. I read Heidegger, especially at this stage of his thought, as wanting to distinguish Dasein both from beings and from Being, a point that can be obscured by the capitalization of "Being" in passages such as this one. (This dilemma of capitalization probably amused Derrida, since it marks a place in which the "nonlinguistic" [typography] plays a key role in how a written text is understood and interpreted. For a fuller explanation of this, see, for example, *Of Grammatology*.)
9. Note "existence," not "its existence," which would raise yet again the question of the status and meaning of the "it."
10. Jacques Taminiaux, in his contribution to *Reading Heidegger from the Start*, "The Husserlian Heritage in Heidegger's Notion of the Self," suggests part of the problem is that in *Being and Time*, Heidegger still sees the project of fundamental ontology as a universal one and, hence, remains too close to Husserl's project (Kisiel and van Buren 1994, 289).
11. On this point, see Dreyfus, *Being-in-the-World*, p. 27; cf. Heidegger *Logic: The Question of Truth*, pp. 190–92.

5 The *Kehre*

This is what *Being and Time* still only glimpsed through a cloud ...

—Jean Beaufret (*Douze Questions*, 1974, my translation)

I: The Basic Problems of Phenomenology

Although Heidegger identifies the 1927 lectures on *The Basic Problems of Phenomenology* as part 3 of division 2 of *Being and Time* (Heidegger 1982, 1, fn), this text, like *Logic: The Question of Truth*, lacks the preoccupation with *Angst* and nullity found in the more famous book written between the two. This may be because, as Albert Hofstadter notes in the translator's preface, these lectures mark the turning point in Heidegger's thought from a preoccupation with Dasein to a focus on Being itself (Heidegger 1982, xi). When Dreyfus first read the English translation of *The Basic Problem of Phenomenology*, he described it to his students as a rethinking of, and improvement on, *Being and Time*.[1] These lectures explore in depth both the temporality of Dasein (chapter 1 of the unfinished part 2) and the problem of consciousness, (chapter 3 of part 1), which explicitly invokes the Cartesian distinction between "*res extensa*" and "*res cogitans.*" This distinction leads, in a way that has become familiar by now, to Dreyfus's observation in "Why Heideggerian AI Failed and How Fixing It Would Require Making It More Heideggerian" that "most basically we are absorbed copers," which means that in the study of consciousness, "the inner-outer distinction becomes problematic" (Dreyfus 2007, 255). After that comment, Dreyfus adds a quotation from the 1922 introduction to the unwritten book on Aristotle, which is less strange than it may seem, because these lectures, in many ways, return to the understanding of human existence laid out in the 1919 lectures, *Toward a Definition of Philosophy*.

The second section of the introduction to *Basic Problems* addresses the relationship between philosophy and "world-views," a discourse Heidegger describes in 1919 as one in which "some solve the ultimate problems by remaining within a dualism of nature and spirit, others trace these two worlds back to one common origin—God—which is itself conceived *extra mundum* or made identical with all Being. Others interpret everything spiritual as natural, mechanical, energetic Being; still others, by contrast, treat nature as spirit." In the face of this view, Heidegger asks, "Or is a quite different, critical, scientific conception of our topic still possible?," where "critical" has specifically Kantian overtones. He clearly states, "Philosophy as critical science is *not identical* with the teaching of a worldview" (Heidegger 2008, 7–9; his emphasis). In 1927, he says unequivocally, "Philosophy is not essentially the formation of a world view." Rather, "We assert now that *being is the proper and sole theme of philosophy*"[2] because "philosophy is ontological. In contrast, a world-view is a positing knowledge of beings and a positing attitude toward beings; it is not ontological, but ontical" (Heidegger 1982, 10–11; his emphasis). There is thus continuity between these texts that shares much with *Being and Time*, but it sets the conversation in a significantly different context.

Much of chapter 1 of the first part of *Basic Problems* focuses on Kant's distinction between the person as knower and as agent. Heidegger argues against Kant's views, again using some of the same vocabulary as in 1919—for example, the importance of comportment in his understanding of human experience. He quotes Kant's own manuscript notes on *The Critique of Pure Reason*: "That is intellectual whose concept is an action," which Heidegger interprets as "The ego is an 'I act' and as such it is intellectual." His main complaint is that Kant did not understand this point "ontologically," but followed Descartes in seeing the ego, the subject, as a thing (Heidegger 1982, 141–42). Heidegger notes, however, that "beginning with a subject-object relation obstructs access to the real ontological question regarding the mode of being of the subject as well as the mode of being of the entity that may possibly but does not necessarily have to become an object.... For an extant entity does not of itself become an object so as then to require a subject; rather it becomes an object only in being objectified *by* a subject" (Heidegger 1982, 157; his emphasis).[3] In other words, according to Heidegger, while Kant recognizes that "nature considered *materialiter* is the *totality of all objects of experience*,"[4] he evades the ontological question of the status of both Dasein and nature by falling back on the Cartesian model of the mental/subjects and the physical/objects. For Heidegger, our relation to nature starts not with subjects and objects, but with a holistic perceptual experience based in a meaningful social world and geared toward action—an empty directedness we are taught to label in various ways as we are taught the options for filling it—out of which the mental and the physical are later abstracted.

Heidegger also makes it clear that such abstraction is an action of that which creates itself as subject in the same act. "To intentionality belongs, not only a self-directing-toward and not only an understanding of the being of the being toward which it is directed, but also *the associated unveiling of the self* which is comporting itself here" (Heidegger 1982, 158; his emphasis). This quotation shows, once again, the implausibility of reading these early works as elaborations, corrections, or variants on intentionality, as it is traditionally understood. In these lectures, Heidegger is relatively explicit in his denials that this is the case, and he emphasizes instead the radicality of his own thought: "It will turn out that intentionality is founded in the Dasein's transcendence and is possible solely for this reason—that transcendence cannot conversely be explained in terms of intentionality" (Heidegger 1982, 162). It should be clear that intentionality without a pre-existing subject or self as its source is as far as possible from both Descartes and Kant. In fact, Heidegger notes that "it must be said that this enigmatic phenomenon of intentionality [which he links to Scholasticism] is far from having been adequately comprehended philosophically." Heidegger believes the key is to divide the "toward which" of intentionality into two elements—the *"whereto of the comporting* and *toward-which of the directedness"*—which he believes the traditional concept of intentionality conflates (Heidegger 1982, 58; his emphasis, my interpolation).

He begins to rethink intentionality in this way by noting that the traditional account of the intentional/perceptual situation depends on the presence of both a perceiver and a perceived. But this implies that "as an isolated subject, this subject is without intentionality." For him, Dasein is always directed toward something. "The intentional relation does not arise first through the actual extantness of objects but lies in the perceiving itself, whether illusionless or illusory. Perceiving must be the perception-of-something in order for me to be able to be deceived *about* something" (Heidegger 1982, 60; his emphasis). This is because "the mode of being of our own self, the Dasein, is essentially such that this being, so far as it *is*, is always already dwelling with the extant" (Heidegger 1982, 64; his emphasis). What ek-sists, as opposed to what is extant, does so precisely because it is directed-toward in this way. "By their essential nature, perceptions relate to something perceived; they point toward or refer to it, but not in such a way that this referential structure would first have to be procured for them; rather, they have it from the start *as* perception. Whether they give correctly what they claim to be giving is another question" (Heidegger 1982, 67; his emphasis). We can see now that the towards-which of intentionality is an essential trait of Dasein that can be distinguished from the whereto of intentionality, which is comportment in the context of a specific project with a specific ontic aim. I can look out my window at the trees to gauge how strong the wind is prior to walking home or to find an example for my argument (the whereto of my comportment). However, my perception of the trees is not the act of a self-subsistent consciousness but is, in the first place, pre-personal (i.e., when I turn my head, my gaze is necessarily grasped by the movement of the branches). This fact reflects the essential towards-which of my existence as Dasein.

Heidegger later adds a third dimension to the towards-which and whereto of intentionality: "To intentionality belong, not only a self-directing-toward and not only an understanding of the being of the being toward which it is directed, but also the *associated unveiling of the self* which is comporting here." This self is not an entity that could be an object for reflection—"The self is there for the Dasein itself without reflection and without inner perceptions, *before* all reflecting." Dasein does not find itself in reflection (where it would become an object of reflection and, thus, no longer itself as reflecting), but rather *"finds itself* primarily and constantly *in things* because, tending them, distressed by them, it always in some way or other rests in things. Each one of us is what he pursues and cares for" (Heidegger 1982, 158–59; his emphasis). In the case just cited, I "am" the being who does not want to be cold walking home and/or the being who wants to make a certain philosophical point.

In contrast to the Existentialists, however, for Heidegger our existence as selves is derived from our existence as Dasein, and our existence as Dasein rests on our lived experience in an already meaningful social world. The philosophical reduction to "self" and "world" cannot deny the fundamental reality of lived experience without destroying the basis of its own theorizing. He made this same point in the 1919 lectures, where he stated, for example, "The genuine solution of the problem of reality of the external world consists in the insight that this is no problem at all, but rather an absurdity" (Heidegger 2008, 71). In *Being and Time*, he said, "The 'problem of Reality' in the sense of the question of whether an external world is present-at-hand and whether such a world can be proved, turns out to be an impossible one, not because its consequences lead to inextricable impasses, but because the very entity which serves as its theme, is one which, as it were, repudiates any such formulation of the question" (Heidegger 1962, 250).

Perception understood as a world of pre-existing and fixed material objects encountered by a pre-existing and fixed subject must be rethought. Trees and wind do not first exist for me, then become objects of my concern, but the reverse. "Original familiarity with beings lies in *dealing with them* appropriately" (Heidegger 1982, 304; his emphasis). That is, the world must be understood as a realm in which an upsurge of beings (φύσις) appears in the context of questions asked and answered in a way focused, in the first place, on action by an entity that itself becomes what it is in this interchange. For Heidegger, that is the only way to avoid the epistemological paradoxes and skepticism, not to say nihilism, generated by Descartes's mind/body dualism. He notes that "the theories of relativism and skepticism spring from a partially justified opposition to an absurd absolutism and dogmatism of the concept of truth" (Heidegger 1982, 222).

Basic Problems can also be seen as a transition point between the early lectures, with their preoccupation with Aristotle and *Being and Time* on the one hand, and the two key texts on truth from the 1930s on the other. Addressing the meaning of the verb "to be" in chapter 4, he cites Kant, Husserl, and others as not succeeding "in conceiving logic philosophically" (Heidegger 1982, 178), and he traces the history of the problem of "is" as the copula in an effort to "elucidate what being-true means and how it stands in regard to the Dasein" (Heidegger 1982, 183). His conclusion is, "The problem of the copula is difficult and intricate not because inquiry into it takes its start in general from the logos but because this phenomenon of the logos as a whole has been inadequately assured and circumscribed" (Heidegger 1982, 205). He begins retracing this error, as usual, with Plato, specifically the "Sophist." Heidegger notes, "Plato arrives at the knowledge that...every assertion [is] an assertion *about* something. This is seemingly trivial and yet it is a puzzle." Heidegger summarizes his earlier discussion about intentionality by saying, "*Intentional comportment* in the sense of *assertion* about something is *founded* in its *ontological structure* in the basic constitution of the Dasein which we described as *being-in-the-world*.... And not only is this being with which the Dasein dwells uncovered but that being which is the Dasein itself is also at the same time unveiled" (Heidegger 1982, 208; his emphasis, my interpolation). On this basis, he concludes, "Being-true is *extant* neither in things nor in a mind. On the other hand, however, truth as unveiling is in the Dasein as a determination of its intentional comportment." For this reason, "There is truth—unveiling and unveiledness—only when and as long as Dasein exists" because "truth belongs to the ontological constitution of the Dasein itself" (Heidegger 1982, 218–20; his emphasis). Thus, the key to understanding our own existence as consciousness and our relation to the beings around us (and Being itself) can be found in the essence of truth.

II: Metaphysics, Being, and Truth

The last of Heidegger's unfinished lectures on *The Basic Problems of Phenomenology* was to be on "the problem of the *truth-character of being*" (Heidegger 1982, 225; his emphasis). He fulfilled that implicit promise in a paper titled "On the Essence of Truth" and in the lecture course at Freiberg University that was published as *The Essence of Truth*. These two texts represent the core of the argument of the present book, which marks the point in Heidegger's work where his early thinking about our relationship with things around us and our nature as Dasein comes into focus as the radical new beginning it is. Only after writing a shorter version of this present argument[5] did I read the interview with Jean Beaufret, in which he responds to a question about why Heidegger never completed the second part of *Being and Time*: "One can say that these twenty pages [of "On the Essence of Truth"] constitute the pattern [*filigrane*, filigree, but also watermark] behind all Heidegger's later work" (Beaufret 1974, 28; my interpolation). Beaufret traces this pattern in terms of history and *Ereignis*, or the event, but I will follow the thread previously cited that leads from Being to the truth of Being.[6] However, it will be helpful to first offer a brief, if nonstandard, interpretation of Heidegger's inaugural address to the Freiburg University faculties in 1929, "What is Metaphysics?" This discussion will establish the connections between freedom, nothingness, and the open, and it will reveal a link between Heidegger and Aristotle that clearly shows how far Heidegger's use of these terms is from the common existentialist readings of the two lectures and, by extension, of *Being and Time*.

As was the case with the early lectures considered in chapter 3, "What is Metaphysics?" is set in the context of the university and, specifically, of the relationship between science and the humanities. Heidegger asks, "What happens to us, essentially, in the grounds of our existence, when science becomes our passion?" On a mundane level that question seems at odds with his title question, and it hints at debates within the university that are far from over. He denies that science has any priority among the faculties: "No particular way of treating objects of inquiry dominates the others. Mathematical knowledge is no more rigorous than philological-historical knowledge. It merely has the character of 'exactness,' which does not coincide with rigor. To demand exactness in the study of history is to violate the idea of the specific rigor of the humanities."

This comment leads to the famous discussion of the "nothing,"[7] presented here as a sign of the limits of scientific knowledge that resonates with his statements a decade earlier about the relationship between science and consciousness. In science, he argues, "What should be examined are beings only, and besides that—nothing; beings alone and further—nothing; solely beings and beyond that—nothing."[8] Just as science requires consciousness but refuses to acknowledge its existence as consciousness, "when science tries to express its proper essence it calls upon the nothing for help. It has recourse to what it rejects" (Heidegger 1993, 94–96). We return here to Krell's nullity of Dasein in that beings as a whole (to which the nothing is opposed) are revealed by "anxiety" (*Angst*). "We 'hover' in anxiety," Heidegger explains, "because it induces the slipping away of beings as a whole. This implies that we ourselves—we humans who are in being—in the midst of beings slip away from ourselves. At bottom therefore it is not as though 'you' or 'I' feel ill at ease; rather, it is this way for some 'one'" (Heidegger 1993, 101).[9] The impersonality of this *Angst* is made clear when he states, "The nothing itself nihilates," or more famously and perhaps more accurately, "The nothing nothings" (Heidegger 1993, 103).

Not only is anxiety essentially impersonal, in the sense that we experience it as something anyone can experience (which is part of its anguish), but we are also passive in our relationship to it in that we cannot make the nothing (the meaningless of beings as a whole) reveal itself on our command. "We are so finite that we cannot even bring ourselves originally before the nothing through our own decision and will" (Heidegger 1993, 106). This is because "Da-sein means: *being held* out into the nothing," and our transcendence of beings as a whole consists precisely in this. The nothing, then, is the nonspatial or prespatial space around us which allows us to encounter the things in the world as the meaningful things they are, rather than as stimuli to which we respond in instinctual ways or ways learned through instinctual processes (such as positive reinforcement). "Without the original revelation of the nothing [of our relation to beings as a whole], no selfhood and no freedom." This is because "the nothing makes possible the openedness of beings as such" (Heidegger 193, 103–4, my emphasis and interpolation).

We have already seen how this nothing reveals our freedom, in that we can act or not act, and we can do so for reasons that reveal the goals and meanings we give to our lives. Beyond that, however, the anxiety induced by the nothing is not entirely an existential one in the usual sense, or not entirely so. Yes, it reveals my own internal emptiness, my lack of an essence that would give my life meaning. More basically, however, awareness of the nothing entails awareness of the lack of ontological ground—not only for my existence, but for the meaningful world in which I exist and for the existence of any meaningful world at all. The meanings we find in our lives constitute a sort of linguistic/cultural overlay on a reality to which we have only very limited access. And we have access only insofar as it allows us to act in the world or as it frustrates our attempts to act. For example, scientists may successfully send a probe to Mars, or the probe may malfunction and fail to reach its target.

Given the openedness of the nothing, we are also able to focus on what is discovered there—call it "reality"—and we can lose ourselves in the details of day-to-day life. "The more we turn toward beings in our preoccupations…the more we turn away from nothing. Just as surely do we hasten into the public superficies of existence." Our behavior in such cases is not "mere negation," but it does speak "out in the 'no' and in negation. Indeed here for the first time the barrenness and range of negation betray themselves" (Heidegger 193, 104–5). As we saw in the previous chapter, we are beings who have "powers"—that is, we can act on the world (as can all beings with "souls"), and our powers can have either of two opposite effects (an ability unique to beings with "rational" souls or language users). This means that Dasein introduces negation and emptiness into a world that would otherwise be full of undifferentiated "stuff" moving in predetermined, law-like ways. In another echo of his early lectures, Heidegger notes that things can exist as the things they are only for a being for which they exist as such: "Only in the nothing of Dasein do beings as a whole, in accord with their most proper possibility—that is, in a finite way—come to themselves" (Heidegger 1993, 108).

To summarize, I would argue that there are three dimensions, or meanings, to the nothing in Heidegger's text. The first dimension is the nothing as an ontic experience of Dasein, the source of the lived experience of *Angst*. This nothing puts us in relationship to being as a whole and allows us to live authentically in this relationship, or to flee back into the false security of what "one" believes about the world, as described in part 1 of *Being and Time*.[10] The second dimension is that which makes possible the openedness of beings as such—that which allows us to take them as the beings they are. This is the empty "space" between them and us. The third dimension is that which appears to be new here. As we have seen, for Heidegger, "Da-sein means: *being held* out into the nothing," which means that for Dasein and Dasein alone, things cannot only be or not be—they can also be or not be true. As in Aristotle, in this idea lies our freedom, though in a very different sense than the freedom of existentialism.

While deeply intertwined in Heidegger's texts, I consider these three distinct "dimensions" of the nothing because they can be seen from different perspectives. The first can be seen from the perspective of the lived experience of Dasein (the "whereto" that underlies intentionality). The second can be seen from the perspective of beings (the "towards-which"). The third can be seen from the perspective of what Dasein most primordially is. The nothing, to shift again to Aristotle's terminology, marks us as souls with "discourse," as Heidegger insists in *Aristotle's Metaphysics* Θ 1–3 two years later (hence, the central focus on truth). The nothing is what sets consciousness apart from what occurs from "necessity"—that is, from beings as objects of scientific study. Thus, it makes sense that Heidegger returns at the end of this address to the debate about the primacy of science: "For this reason no amount of scientific rigor attains to the seriousness of metaphysics. Philosophy can never be measured by the standard of the idea of science" (Heidegger 1993, 110).

III: On the Essence of Truth

Truth, Openness and Comportment

Beaufret describes the evolution of Heidegger's thought after *Being and Time* as a shift in perspective: "The forgetting of Being is no longer a simple inadvertence as the reader of *Sein und Zeit* might have believed. It becomes an issue of Being itself, not our being. In other words, in the phrase: *forgetting of Being*, the objective genitive [i.e., our forgetting of Being] is suddenly reversed into a subjective genitive. The forgetting comes from Being" (Beaufret 1974, 27; his emphasis, my translation, my interpolation). This is what precludes a Husserlian or Sartrean interpretation of these later texts, as might still be possible with *Being and Time*. Thomas Sheehan notes, "As William J. Richardson pointed out over fifty years ago, Heidegger's lecture 'On the Essence of Truth'…is the 'decisive point' in Heidegger's development and constitutes the 'breakthrough' in which 'Heidegger I becomes Heidegger II'" (Sheehan 2015, 223). Sheehan also notes that in *Contributions to Philosophy: Of the Event*, Heidegger cites Section 6 of "On the Essence of Truth" as "the point where his thinking first addresses 'the *Kehre* that is at work in appropriation [*Ereignis*]'" (Sheehan 2015, 238; my interpolation).[11]

Although these texts locate the key shift in the lecture "On the Essence of Truth," based on the reading of Heidegger's earlier works presented here, I have come to see the trajectory of Heidegger's thought as much more unified, with *Being and Time* as a detour, rather than a "dead alley" after which his philosophy took a major turn. This means that "On the Essence of Truth" would not be a new start for Heidegger, but rather a circling back, though at a higher level on the hermeneutic circle, to the same conceptual framework he had been building, clarifying, and elaborating from the beginning. We have seen how earlier ideas reappear in "What is Metaphysics?" Next, we will make a similar exploration of this lecture.

Heidegger begins "On the Essence of Truth" with the observation that our everyday use of the word "truth" has two levels: we speak of "true gold in distinction from false" but "above all we call true or false our statements about beings, which can themselves be genuine or not." This conceals the fact that the latter level, "propositional truth," understood as the correspondence of the statement to the facts of the matter, "is possible only on the basis of material truth." The truth of the statement "this ring is gold" depends on the ring being real gold rather than false gold.

This point undermines the apparent reversibility of the two ways of translating the Medieval Latin formula, *veritas est adaequatio rei et intellectūs*: "truth is the correspondence... of the matter to knowledge" and "truth is the correspondence of knowledge to the matter." To our contemporary ears, "truth is the correspondence of the matter to knowledge" sounds peculiar, if not simply wrong. Heidegger traces the formulation backwards in time—first to Kant's claim that "objects correspond to our knowledge" and then to the medieval belief that material objects, as created, must conform to the pre-existing ideas of them in the mind of God. According to this view, human knowledge is based on the ability of our minds to correctly trace the correspondence between the "true things" in the world and those in the mind of God (Heidegger 1993, 118). In the modern world, the supposed self-evidence of the "correspondence theory" of truth remains, but it is based on only half of the medieval formula (the correspondence of our knowledge to matter). "True" gold is now measured in terms of properties such as atomic weight, not in terms of fidelity to a divine idea. Heidegger notes that this is what makes the science of nature, understood as "technical mastery over things," part of technology. However, it is not only with regard to the "divine" that the other side of the definition of truth has been relegated to the scrap heap, but also with regard to what he takes to be the Kantian insight that, as we saw in *Basic Problems*, perception is action-based, not a bare looking at something.

The technological definition of truth gives the impression that the essence of truth "is independent of the interpretation of the essence of the Being of all beings, which always includes a corresponding interpretation of the essence of man as the bearer and executor of *intellectus*." Once knowledge is no longer a correspondence between human and divine ideas, however, a long tradition of skepticism asks how ideas (or propositions) can "correspond" to the "matter," which is neither idea nor word. "But wherein are the thing and the statement supposed to be in accordance, considering that the relata are manifestly different in their outward appearance?" How can the letters *g, o, l*, and *d* or the sound "gold" correspond to a piece of yellow metal? Clearly, "Correspondence here cannot signify a thing-like approximation between dissimilar kinds of things. The essence of the correspondence is determined rather by the kind of relation that obtains between the statement and the thing." Sounds or marks on a paper must in some sense stand in relation to one another as the corresponding things do in the world, "What is stated by the presentative statement is said of the presented thing in just such manner *as* that thing, as presented, is," where to present "means to let the thing stand opposed as object."

The statement "This is gold" is true only when it presents an object that is in fact gold. But this shifts the focus from the object to the conditions of its presentation. "This appearing of the thing in traversing a field of opposedness takes place within an open region, the openness of which is not first created by the presenting, but rather is only entered into and taken over as a domain of relatedness" (Heidegger 1993, 119–21; his emphasis). I would like to offer two comments here. First, the field of opposedness corresponds to the "openedness" that we saw can be understood as one dimension of the nothing in "What is Metaphysics?" Second, the impersonality of this open region and our passivity in relation to it provide evidence for the shift Beaufret sees in this lecture, from a focus on "our being" to a focus on Being itself.

The link with the earlier works becomes clearer when Heidegger returns to comportment: "The relation of the presentative statement to the thing is the accomplishment of that *bearing* [*Verhältnis*] which originally and always comes to prevail as a comportment [*Verhalten*]." Objects draw our attention because of the use we can make of them and the way they fit into our projects in a social world; they are what we are looking for in the situations in which they are encountered. "Comportment stands open to beings." Our "bearing" toward something that presents itself as gold will be different if we are searching for a metal to make an axe than if we are searching for a metal of monetary worth, and the truth of the claim that it is gold will also carry a correspondingly different weight. "Truth does not originally reside in the proposition." Rather, it resides in "this openness of comportment" toward what in our surroundings is needed to complete it.[12] "To free oneself for a binding directedness is possible only by *being free* for what is opened up in an open region." A human with an injured foot, for example, will have his or her attention grabbed by a fallen tree branch in a way that an injured guinea pig will not. The openedness of the nothing is the condition of our freedom, our power to make things be or not be, and, thus, it is the condition of our existence as human consciousness: "*The essence of truth is freedom.*" But this seems to make truth dependent on human consciousness. The metaphysical tradition "regards such truth as imperishable and eternal, which can never be founded on the transitoriness and fragility that belong to man's essence." So the question of truth brings us back to the question of our existence as humans, as "man." This is a problem precisely because "everyone knows what man is" (Heidegger 1993, 121–24; his emphasis).

Truth and Freedom

If freedom, "as freedom for what is opened up in an open region," is an essential aspect of our existence as Dasein, it is also true that freedom, in that sense, "lets beings be the beings they are." That is, our freedom allows the being of beings to be disclosed as the beings that they are, which for Heidegger is the core meaning of the Greek word for truth, alētheia, which can be literally translated as "uncon-cealment" or "disclosedness." One reason for regarding this text as pivotal is that, in this section and elsewhere, Heidegger connects the question of truth to the problem of technological modernity, rather than to the status of science in the university. "To let things be," he warns us, "does not refer to neglect and indif-ference but rather the opposite. To let be is to engage oneself with beings. On the other hand, to be sure, this is not to be understood as the mere management, preservation, tending, and planning of the beings." Heidegger is not speaking of either Dreyfus's "absorbed coping" of day-to-day life or of science geared toward putting things to technological use, but of an engagement "with the open region and its openness into which every being comes to stand, bringing that openness, as it were, along with itself."

It can help here to remember that Aristotle was more a natural historian than a scientist in the modern sense. He observed (or had others observe for him) rather than manipulating nature to reveal its secrets, as the modern sci-entist is advised. "To engage oneself with the disclosedness of beings is not to lose oneself in them; rather, such engagement withdraws in the face of beings in order that they might reveal themselves with respect to what and how they are, and in order that presentative correspondence [of truth] might take its standard from them." This is the scientific method of Einstein and Bohr, rather than of the Curies (or, perhaps, Edelman).

But the main topic here is the relationship between freedom and truth. About that, Heidegger states, "Considered in regard to the essence of truth, the essence of freedom manifests itself as exposure to the disclosedness of beings." This means that freedom cannot be "caprice," "freedom from restraint," or "mere readiness for what is required and necessary," that is, not otherwise in use, freedom in the sense that a taxi is "free." He adds, "Prior to all this ('nega-tive' and 'positive' freedom), freedom is engagement in the disclosure of beings as such. Disclosedness itself is conserved in ek-sistent engagement, through which the openness of the open region, i.e., the 'there' ['*Da*'], is what it is." We are free because beings appear in our field of disclosedness in ways that allow us, primarily, to make use of them (or not) and, secondarily, to see them as things of certain kinds. Historically, the grouping of things into kinds (i.e., seeing them as the things they are) is derived from the ways in which we make use of them. In Plato's "Sophist," for example, sea birds are grouped with fish and aquatic mammals, while land birds are grouped with land animals. Those groupings reflect a type of folk taxonomy[13] that depends on the human relationships to different kinds of birds (i.e., "absorbed copers" for whom meat was "unready-to-hand" found that, while land birds were be shot with arrows like rabbits, aquatic birds could more easily be netted out of the water like fish). This folk system contrasts with our familiar scientific system of genus, species, and other taxonomic groups, derived from Aristotelian natural history, which focuses on the biological relationships among the animals themselves. Those biological relationships allow us to group sea eagles with land raptors and whales with hippopotamuses.

Note here that freedom and the open are linked to the core existence of Dasein, its location in an historical time and place, its "Da." Moreover, Heidegger goes on immediately to differentiate this concept of ek-sistence as being held out into the nothing from existence understood as "man's moral endeavor on behalf of his 'self,' based on his psychophysical constitution," that is, one could argue, from existence understood as it is in existentialist interpretations of *Being and Time*. He also notes that human "caprice" does not have freedom "at its disposal. Man does not possess freedom." Rather, "freedom, ek-sistent, disclosive Da-sein, possesses man."

But freedom gives us not only the general possibility to do or not to do, but also the specific possibility of not letting "beings be the beings which they are and as they are. Then beings are covered up and distorted." Thus, freedom opens the possibility of falsity, both in the sense in which an object can appear to be what it is not and in the sense in which *intellectus* can falsely predicate of an object what is not true of it. However, falsity is not a secondary phenomenon caused by "human incapacity and negligence." Rather, "truth and untruth are, *in essence, not* irrelevant to one another, but belong together" (Heidegger 1993, 125–28; his emphasis, my interpolations). This explains the internal link between the Greek word for truth, a-lētheia, and it's opposite, *lētheia*. To understand the essence of truth, we must also understand the essence of untruth, both as *pseudos* (falsity) and as what is undisclosed.

Untruth

At this point, Heidegger reminds us that truth as disclosedness exists for us primarily as an "attunement" to the world of our daily lives as Dreyfus' "absorbed copers"—that is, we exist in a world of meanings out of which specific truths can appear to us as such. The most efficient way to hit a nail is not a "truth" to a carpenter until she is asked why she uses her hammer in the way she does. "Being attuned, i.e., ek-sistent exposedness to beings as a world, can be 'experienced' and 'felt' only because the 'man who experiences,' without being aware of the essence of the attunement, is always engaged in being attuned in a way that discloses being as a whole" (Heidegger 1993, 129). In our daily absorption in our world, things as a whole are revealed in terms of the meanings available in that world and from the perspective of that world. To twist a famous saying, to a person with a sledge hammer, beings reveal themselves as things to be smashed. Or in the contemporary university, to a person with a spreadsheet, things reveal themselves as data. At the same time, under normal conditions, things that are not of immediate relevance to the task at hand are not revealed at all. Remember the chalk and the board that Heidegger is unaware of during his absorption in writing.

There is a more insidious way in which beings as a whole can recede from us. Heidegger hints at a third kind of untruth beyond the false and the undisclosed when he refers to the modern technological age as one "where the familiar and well-known has becomes boundless, and nothing is any longer able to withstand the business of knowing, since technical mastery over things bears itself without limit. Precisely in the leveling and planning of this omniscience, this mere knowing, the openedness of beings gets flattened out into the apparent nothingness of what is no longer even a matter of indifference, but rather is simply forgotten" (Heidegger 1993, 129). Technology carries the risk of leading to a time when there will be only one "world," and when Dasein will no longer be held out into the nothing but will instead be bound into the being of beings understood as "standing reserve."

Of the three forms of untruth, the concealed or undisclosed is "most proper to *alētheia* as its own," but it also opens the way to the other forms of untruth. In daily life, freedom discloses beings as the beings they are on the basis of our comportment toward them (i.e., whether and how they are thematically or implicitly present to us in what we do), but it also "conceals itself in the process, letting a forgottenness of the mystery take precedence and disappearing in it." We not only are unaware of the sledgehammer as we swing it or the spreadsheet as we fill in data, but we also take as ultimate what is derivative—the sledgehammer or the spreadsheet determines how we understand the task. It is easier to destroy things than to fix them, easier to measure and calculate than to understand the phenomena represented by the numbers. "Man clings to what is readily available and controllable even where ultimate matters are concerned," yet "the forgotten mystery of Dasein" still haunts this world. That is why in the technological age, phenomena come to be identified in terms of numbers. "Progress" is not a matter of whether people are better off, but of how many old buildings we can knock down and replace with new ones. Learning is no longer measured by test scores, rather test scores "prove" whether learning has happened. Thus, almost the full critique of the technological age is already present in this text:

> Thus left, humanity replenishes its 'world' on the basis of the latest needs and aims, and fills out that world by means of proposing and planning. From these man then takes his standards, forgetting being as a whole. He persists in them and continually supplies himself with new standards, yet without considering either the ground for taking up standards or the essence of what gives the standard.... He is all the more mistaken the more exclusively he takes himself, as subject, to be the standard of all beings.

This is what Heidegger calls "errancy."

As the translator points out, errancy, in this context, is more closely connected to the idea of a "knight errant," a wandering knight, than to the concept of error, though the wandering is not necessarily an innocent wandering about as much as it is a wandering unconstrained by the control of a nobleman. For Heidegger, "errancy belongs to the inner constitution of the Da-sein into which historical man is admitted" and "every mode of comportment has its mode of erring." Knights can wander off the path, but so can teachers and administrators or construction workers and engineers—each in a way connected to a specific "world" and their place in it. Our normal (and even philosophical) sense of incorrectness and falsity are "only one mode of erring and, moreover, the most superficial one." Rather, "errancy dominates man through and through." This is because our ek-sistence is made possible by our freedom, which itself "originates from the primordial essence of truth, the rule of the mystery in errancy." Our natural path as "absorbed copers" takes us away from the truth of our situation and toward what is most obvious and available. We are intrinsically directed outwards, toward the world, and we understand ourselves in terms of it. But when we turn away from Being to beings, we lose our access to what we most primordially are. At this point, Heidegger turns briefly to the other pole of his thought after the *Kehre*, the history of philosophy from the ancient Greeks—"The thinking of Being...has since Plato been understood as 'philosophy,' and later received the title 'metaphysics'"—to Kant, "whose work introduces the final turning of Western metaphysics" and finally links truth back to Being (Heidegger 1993, 129–36).

To summarize, our freedom as beings "with discourse" puts us at a distance from beings that act or function by necessity. The open field that our ability to do or not do discloses beings as the beings they are. But due to errancy, we engage with them primarily as needed for day-to-day comportment, where they are truly or falsely what they appear to be based on what we take them for. We can also speak of them truly or falsely, but only derivatively. The "open field of opposedness" discloses not only the beings we encounter, but also "beings as a whole," as Aristotle said of φύσις (Heidegger 1993, 126). Taken in conjunction with the lectures on Aristotle's *Physics* discussed in chapter 1, in which "wherever a being from φύσις stands in the open, φύσις has already shown itself and stands in view" (Heidegger 1995, 240), this interpretation suggests a way to make sense of the claim in *Introduction to Metaphysics* that "*phusis* is Being itself" (Heidegger 2000, 14–15). If, as Heidegger argues, "the disclosure of beings as such is simultaneously and intrinsically the concealing of being as a whole," then the concealment or forgetting of Being is the condition of things being disclosed as such—that is, physis as the upsurge or source of all that is. Things appear to us out of the hiddenness or forgetting of beings as a whole through the upsurge of physis, but primarily as what is or is not relevant in everyday comportment. As Beaufret notes, the focus here is no longer on our forgetting of Being, but on Being as what is (self-)concealed, what withdraws from explicit awareness. "The essence of truth is not the empty 'generality' of an 'abstract' universality but rather that which, self-concealing, is unique in the unremitting history of the disclosure of the 'meaning' of what we call Being—what we for a long time have been accustomed to considering only as being as a whole."

In terms of the trajectory of Heidegger's thought, I'd like to point out that the "Note" added to this lecture over a decade later states, "Our thinking apparently remains on the path of metaphysics. Nevertheless, in its decisive steps, which lead from truth as correctness to ek-sistent freedom, and from the latter to truth as concealing and as errancy [that is, in "On the Essence of Truth"], it accomplishes a change in the questioning that belongs to the overcoming of metaphysics" (Heidegger 1993, 130–38; my interpolation). Two observations can be made here. First, if he regards this lecture as still "on the path of metaphysics," how much more must that be the case for *Being and Time*? Secondly, the Note suggests that Heidegger himself saw "On the Essence of Truth" as the locus for "a change in the questioning" that guides the rest of his work.

Notes

1. Based on personal experience/memory.
2. Again, the translator of this texts uses "being" where others might use "Being." As above, I will follow his usage in quotations, but use Being in my text for consistency.
3. Almost the same formulation appears in the lectures on Aristotle's *Physics* a dozen years later (Heidegger 1999, 227).
4. *Prolegomena to Any Future Metaphysics* (Kant 2001, 36, Kant's emphasis).
5. See "Nature (or Not) in Heidegger" in *Ontologies of Nature: Continental Perspectives and Environmental Reorientations*.

6. For more on *Ereignis* in Heidegger and its relationship to the present argument, see Holland's *The Madwoman's Reason* (1998).

7. It is extremely helpful in following Heidegger's argument here (and elsewhere) to keep in mind that the German for the nothing, "*das Nichts*," carries a direct allusion to "*nicht*" and hence implies an active nihilation (the not[h]ing that is completely lost, if it ever existed, in the more static English word (no-thing).

8. I cannot let pass without comment the poetic use of iteration for emphasis here; one wonders how it sounded when he read it aloud in German.

9. This translator also uses "being" in the singular for "Being."

10. This may explain why Heidegger seems to believe authenticity is possible as a constant state. It is not an attitude but a way of relating to things as a whole that seems closer to my concept of "ontological humility" than I realized at the time I wrote that book. By contrast, authenticity, or good faith, as an active attitude seems to be at most a momentary and partial escape from the tyranny of the "They," as Sartre argues. This is another example of a disagreement between the two that hinges on the different levels at which they engage with our lived experience.

11. Several others give this lecture special importance as a transition point in Heidegger's thought, including Jean-Luc Nancy (Nancy 1993, 40), Frederick Olafson (Olafson 1987, 161), and David Farrell Krell in his introductory comments to "On the Essence of Truth" (Heidegger 1993, 112).

12. Cf. the similar discussion of Windelband in chapter 3.

13. This concept is borrowed from Lévi-Strauss's *The Savage Mind*.

6 The Essence of Truth

"The mind is no longer set apart but springs up beside gestures and words as if by spontaneous generation."

—Maurice Merleau-Ponty (*Signs* 1964)

I: *The Essence of Truth*: Truth and Zombies

If the paper "On the Essence of Truth" remains somewhat unclear on the connection between the "mental" and the "physical," on the one hand, and the essence of truth, on the other, the 1932 lectures published as *The Essence of Truth* do not share that vagueness.[1] Before reading through that text, however, I would like to note that there are four levels of truth in Heidegger's thought (though the first two can be combined, for those who prefer the threesomes in these texts). There is material truth (the object *is* gold); propositional truth ("This is gold"); assumed background truths (cf., as noted in chapter 1, Thomas Kuhn's concept of "normal science," but also recent discourse on "epistemologies of ignorance"); and the basic truth of a historic people as revealed in its art (e.g., a religion/culture based on "the essential sacrifice," as we will see in "Origin of the Work of Art" [Heidegger 1993, 187] vs. the gratitude Nietzsche found in the ancient Greeks [Nietzsche 1966, 64]).[2] The different levels are relevant because these lectures are divided into two main parts: a discussion of "The Four Stages of the Occurrence of Truth" in Plato's *Republic*, and "An Interpretation of Plato's 'Theaetetus' With Respect to the Question of the Essence of Untruth." The four stages Heidegger discusses in the Cave Allegory do not exactly correspond to the four levels of truth, though there are resonances between the first three in Plato and the four (or three) in Heidegger with regard to the importance or "reality" of each successive stage.

The stages of truth that Heidegger finds in the *Republic* are the shadows in the Cave, the images in the Cave, the real things outside the Cave, and the return to the Cave. Initially, life in the Cave bears a surprising resemblance to the everyday life and comportment of Dasein: "man straight forwardly takes whatever presents itself before him as un-hidden, to be being; indeed man is nothing else but *the* being that comports itself to what it takes as beings." Heidegger adds, parenthetically, "(an animal, plant, even less a stone never comports itself to beings)" (Heidegger 2002a, 21; his emphasis). This initial stage is the level of truth in the usual sense. The next stage—the unshackling that allows the prisoners to see the imitation objects whose shadows they saw earlier, as well as the fire that cast the shadows—is not much closer to the "Truth" because the freed prisoner only sees the material imitations as different from the shadows without recognizing the relationship between them. That is, we can become aware of the level of what is now called "social construction" (e.g., the social construction of race) without understanding how it shapes what we take to be "true" (e.g., how the racial structure of our social world affects our beliefs and our interactions with others).[3] For Heidegger, "Removal of the shackles is thus not genuine emancipation, for it remains external and fails to penetrate to man in his ownmost self" (Heidegger 2002a, 28). Unshackling frees us *from*, but does not free us *for*. To be free "for" requires awareness of the light by which we see, but, not for Heidegger, the light of the sun. He turns, rather, to the German word for "clearing"—"*lichtung*," or "lighting."

The light creates the clearing, the empty space, or the nothing within which we encounter objects through our comportment in the world. "In this comportment I am able to be *authentically* free, i.e., I can acquire power by *binding* myself to what lets-through"—that is, I can recognize the clearing, the field of opposedness as the source and condition of possibility of my interactions with things, rather than taking things in themselves as primary. In terms reminiscent of *Being and Time*, I become free when I bind myself to the light—to the Being of beings—rather than to beings themselves (Heidegger 2002a, 43–44). Again, the contrast is with science—"the beings which are today the object of theoretical physics are not made *more beingful* through this science, but just the reverse." On the other hand, in a telling addition to the rhetoric here, "the artist possesses essential insight for the possible, for bringing out the inner possibilities of beings, thus for making man see what it really is with which he so blindly busies himself" (Heidegger 2002a, 46–47; his emphasis).

The concept of care is correspondingly redefined: "To be deconcealing is the innermost accomplishment of liberation. It is *care* [*Sorge*] itself: becoming-free as binding oneself to the ideas, as letting *being* give the lead" (Heidegger 2002a, 53; his emphasis).[4] Here, care and authenticity are not attitudes that we can take toward ourselves and others, but a relationship between Dasein and Being. "Truth is neither somewhere *over* man (as validity in itself), nor is it in man as a psychical subject, but man is '*in' the truth*." Conversely, "the question is what truth *itself* is. The first step toward understanding this *question* is the insight that man comes to himself, and finds the *ground* of his Dasein, in that event of deconcealment which constitutes the unhiddenness of being" (Heidegger 2002a, 5; his emphasis). Thus, the fact that we are "possessed" by truth is the essence of what we are.

At the same time, "Untruth *belongs* to the essence of truth" (Heidegger 2002a, 66). We already saw this in "On the Essence of Truth"—"untruth must derive from the essence of truth" (Heidegger 1993, 128). This is the insight at the core of his investigation of Plato's "Theaetetus" in the second part of these lectures. There, he again emphasizes the connection between truth and ontology for the ancient Greeks: truth is alētheia, "the unconcealed," because for them what is true is what is "present, therefore [because existence is defined in terms of presence] existing" (Heidegger 2002a, 103; my interpolation). He argues that "Theaetetus" is not an inconclusive argument about how to identify true propositions, but rather a contribution to fundamental ontology, an account of what it means for something to exist as present. This idea links the dialogue with the question of "how man is to understand himself in his fundamental activity of knowing-his-way-around in things." This question, Heidegger suggests, sets the stage for all subsequent philosophy and binds historical Dasein (in Europe) to a specific interpretation of the essence of truth (Heidegger 2002a, 114–15).

Heidegger, however, is interested in another direction in which the argument in "Theaetetus" might be taken—one directly relevant to the problem of consciousness. In answer to Socrates' question "What is knowledge?," Theaetetus answers "perception." Heidegger follows Plato in inquiring into how the different sense organs are related to our lived experience (e.g., eyes to visual qualities, ears to sounds). The sense organs are the anatomical structures through which the qualities are perceived, but this fact leads to the impossibility of a unified perception based on such disparate experiences. Thus, "*who* is it that sees and hears?" (Heidegger 2002a, 122–24). "We do not see colour in our eyes," Heidegger answers, "and we do not hear sounds in our ears, but rather—where then? Perhaps in the brain? Or perhaps somewhere in a soul which haunts the body like a goblin and runs from one sense-organ to another? We perceive colour, sound, etc., nowhere 'inside', neither in the body nor in the soul, but 'outside'. But what does that mean?" (Heidegger 2002a, 126). For Plato, he says, the perceptual object belongs "to the circle of present things that surround us, and of which we can say it is one and the same space," but "the region from which the perceivable so to speak springs out, is itself, even if the perceivable is *in* space, no longer anything spatial." It is, rather, that on the basis of which perceived space exists for us. It is the openedness, the nothing within which we, as Dasein, live.

In an echo of the persistent anti-scientism found throughout Heidegger's work, he notes that the fact that the perceivable creates the possibility of space, not the other way around, "is not of any lesser importance because it can and must be demonstrated without any scientific instruments and experiments." Perhaps more relevantly, "This *single* pre-given region of possible perceivability, says Plato, one could, if one wishes, call 'soul'" (Heidegger 2002a, 127; his emphasis). What "animates" the human body is not something about us, but rather the meaningful world in which we find ourselves and which elicits our actions from us. This provides a broader answer to the question about the unity of the senses, because "the soul, conceived in this way, is in itself *relational*, it reaches out to … and as such it is already a possible intermediate between which eye, ear, etc., can now be interpolated" (Heidegger 2002a, 128; his ellipsis). As he has argued all along, we reach out to the entities revealed by the openedness around us to answer the question that drives our comportment; thus we unify the senses in the process of using them. If I walk to a street corner, my forward progress down the street requires an answer to the question of whether I need to let cars pass first. Hearing and seeing a car contribute to my awareness of its position and speed, and, hence, are combined into the impression of the same object because they are part of the answer I need about the car. Scientific understanding in terms of vision, hearing, and other senses as distinct modalities is a secondary, privative account of our unified experience of perception based on our comportment in the world.

That Heidegger is referring to something more profound than intentionality as usually understood is clear when he says, "We do not perceive colour and sound because we see and hear, but the reverse"—that is, the object draws us to it as that for which we were looking, rather than being the inert pole of our disinterested looking behavior. As I near a corner, I will notice a car heading toward me at top speed, even if I was not looking for it and even though I can probably avoid the danger it presents by remaining on the sidewalk. He adds, "It is therefore the relationality of the self which makes it possible for the corporeal to be structured organically. Only in this way can a corporeal structure be a *body*. Something can be a body in the proper sense only in so far as it is rooted in a soul." My body is one thing because it functions as a whole in my behavior—legs walking or not, eyes and ears attuned to the traffic, often without any conscious intervention on my part (though, as Edelman notes, the behavior of street-crossing could not have been learned in the first place without some level of consciousness). My glasses or my pen are *almost* a part of my body because they function in the same way, but they are easily removable. My soul, Aristotle tells us, is the "form" of my body—that is, it makes the unified body the entity that it is.

Heidegger also emphasizes the reciprocal fact that "the relationship is the soul itself. It is not firstly soul on its own account, and then, in addition, a relationship to things" (Heidegger 2002a, 129; his emphasis). What does this mean? Consider the zombies we discussed earlier. Traditional zombies, such as those in voodoo culture, were controlled by the necromancer who created them and commanded them to move around and carry out his orders. However, twentieth- and twenty-first-century pop-culture zombies are usually the result of some cataclysm, natural or man-made; they are no longer motivated by the orders of their master, but by their own hunger for human flesh. But why do those movie zombies need to eat flesh, if they are already dead? Because without hunger, "desire," or some vestige of a soul to comport itself toward the world, there would be nothing questionable, no "relationality," and no reason for them to do anything at all. As "souls," we exist and comport ourselves in relationship to the things around us and, because of that, we have perceptions and can move about in the world. Thus, the scientific account of how we perceive is always derivative from our being as "soul." Ultimately, Heidegger interprets Plato as saying, "The soul is what holds up a region of sight within which everything sensibly perceivable is extended" (Heidegger 2002a, 166). If completely without soul, zombies have no perceptual space in which things might appear to them. Only their insatiable hunger engages them with, and organizes, their sensory world.

II: *The Essence of Truth*: Ontology, Not Intentionality

So far, we have seen little that might not appear in the work of more traditional phenomenologists, such as Maurice Merleau-Ponty, or in some forms of American Pragmatism. Heidegger has given us a more complex understanding of intentionality, but one might argue that he is still speaking of nature, perception, and knowledge as usually understood. Yet, Heidegger undermines such an interpretation by insisting on the ontological significance of what he is saying, particularly on the connection for Plato between truth and Being. This can be seen in Heidegger's discussion of false belief, which hints at the distinction between sense (or concept) and reference: "Instead of seeing that [belief] has only *one* object, which, however, possesses a complex rather than a simple unity, and that this complexity is the genuine problem, the prevailing view is always that the object of [belief] consists of two objects [i.e., the concept and the referent]" (Heidegger 2002a, 202; my interpolations). This distinction implies that the concept and the referent are not, in the normal case, entirely independent variables. We saw earlier that the object of an intentional state is that which must be the case for it to be true—the fact that I see a dog is not externally related to the actual presence of a dog. Furthermore, an overemphasis on unicorns and the morning star/evening star in teaching the sense/reference distinction has obscured the fact that the distinction between the concept and referent is a solution to a specific logical (and only secondarily philosophical) problem, rather than a primordial fact about our experience of the world. As my students often point out to me, unicorns *do* exist in books, television shows, and greeting cards, and those who thought that Venus was two different "stars" were simply wrong. Although the "prevailing view" offers one way of interpreting Plato's "Theaetetus," Heidegger suggests that this interpretation may not be the most useful or most correct one.

In "Theaetetus," Plato offers images of the soul, first as a wax tablet on which image-memories are imprinted, then as an aviary full of flying memories we can grab and use as needed. Neither of those images satisfies Socrates in his attempt to understand how we can have false knowledge. Socrates finally asks what a thing and our idea of it have in common. This question leads Heidegger to conclude that Plato's focus is not on memory, but on representation, "the *essence* of making-present, i.e., what first makes something like memory necessary and possible." According to Plato's view, false belief is a making-present based on "mere representation, words, opinions" (concepts) without any genuine relationship to what is made-present (Heidegger 2002a, 212–13). In other words, false belief would be not a substitution of one thing for another similar thing (e.g., the young Socrates for Theaetetus), but a confusion of concepts and referents (e.g., attributing the concept "Socrates" to a referent who is Theaetetus).[5]

Heidegger brings this implicit discussion back to his earlier account of our perception of the natural world, but only after noting that "the usual starting point of epistemology, which asks after an object, after something given, is erroneous" because knowledge is directed not at things but at action.[6] He returns to the idea of comportment, our behavior in relationship to the world around us, and the "peculiar" fact that we can comport ourselves toward beings we do not perceive or do not have explicitly in mind. For example, I can follow a familiar path without thinking about it. These same tacitly perceived beings can also become explicit objects of awareness—as when I turn a corner and discover road repair has closed the sidewalk I usually use, so I must pick another path.

At this point, the account of sense and reference gets turned, first into an epistemological claim, and then into an ontological one. The epistemological claim is that "there are *two* ways in which every being accessible to us can stand, and be had, in our presence"—as actually present (usually called the referent) or as "made present" through memory (the representation or "concept"). "Making present" is crucial for truth because it can be done in two ways: as "an actual enactment of making-present" (e.g., a mental image of the path ahead) or as "a mere awareness of its possibility" (e.g., the lack of surprise when one turns a corner). Most importantly, "What we know in the mode of having-present we can *also* know in the mode of making-present, and what we know in this latter way we may in a given case also *not* know, because we do not have the possibility of having it bodily present." I can be wrong about the path around the bend when relying on my memory in ways I cannot be wrong when I have it visually in front of me. Heidegger draws the conclusion that there are "modes of comportment between knowing and not-knowing, and indeed, which is decisive, in respect of one and the same thing." It is human comportment that determines what is known and not known, true and not true, rather than states of things in the world. This does not mean that "man" is the measure. Rather, the questions "man" asks are in the first place not abstract ones. They arise in our everyday lives when we encounter an "unready-to-hand" that obstructs our forward progress on our current project. As in Heidegger's interpretation of Windelband in 1919, truth requires a being that can judge the fit between the question asked and the answer given by the world in which that being lives.[7]

The ontological claim is interwoven with this epistemological one in Heidegger's text. He notes that, given his account of memory, "the relationship to being (which is what constitutes the soul) not only goes beyond what is perceived, but ... every accessible being can enter into this wider region of attainable beings" (Heidegger 2002a, 218–19; his emphasis). That is, perception potentially opens us up to beings as a whole, or beings that are potentially present and therefore, for the Greeks, potentially exist. He then offers, "naturally with great reservation," a diagram that he characterizes as "a scaffolding around the phenomenon, a scaffolding that must be torn down immediately." I will not try to recreate the diagram here, but its main point seems to be that there is a unitary source for having present (perception) and making present, and this source reaches beyond the present to assert what we cannot yet "see," thus opening the possibility of both truth and error. Without this "reaching beyond," there would be states of affairs but no truth, because perception would simply be what it is. This state is likely the case for some kinds of animals. For Dasein, however, it is possible "to see someone approaching in the distance *as* ...; or e.g. to make-present this approaching person in advance as Theaetetus, who could very well be coming." Or perhaps he is not coming. This two-pronged "fork" is "the condition of the possibility of untruth but at the same time the condition of the possibility of truth." It is also "the image of the fundamental constitution of human Dasein, of its essential construction." It reflects our existence as empty and erring. Making-present opens the possibility of error by "seeing" more than is given, resulting in our mistaking the approaching person for Theaetetus, but it is intrinsic to our ability to recognize the person as the young Socrates when he comes closer. We do not substitute the image of Theaetetus for that of Socrates. Instead, we judge before we have enough information, determining who is approaching by "looking past" what is given in immediate perception (Heidegger 2002a, 222–25).

What "looking past" looks at, however, is actually there. It is not an illusion, but a hiddenness of who is approaching. The person or thing shows itself through hiding itself, so it is both concealed and revealed. It is "a truth to whose essence there belongs un-truth." On this basis, Heidegger elaborates the diagram of the "fork" to show that any given case of error takes place against the background of comportment that is always directed toward Being.[8] We look beyond because we are not reactive beings who must always respond or not respond in the same way. Rather, we are "free" beings who can do or not do or do otherwise. A frog will always respond to large, looming creatures by fleeing, but we have the option of judging the degree of danger of approaching creatures or individuals before we react. The difference between danger and safety is significantly important to our well-being, so we do not want to wait until it is close enough to see clearly. We look beyond what we can see or hear to have time to avoid what might be a life-threatening delay in acting. But this background directedness of Dasein's comportment also allows us to "strive" toward the disclosure of Being. Thus, we might mis-take Being in the same way and by the same mechanism by which we can mis-take Theaetetus for Socrates, or a bison for a bear. "Untruth belongs to the most primordial essence of truth as the hiddenness of being [Being], i.e., to the inner possibility of truth" (Heidegger 2002a, 227–29, my interpolation).

These lectures offer much of the same account of our existence as conscious (or "ensouled") beings that we have found throughout Heidegger's work. However, they undermine traditional philosophy/metaphysics in a much more radical way. The section on the *Republic* includes a cryptic parenthetical note from the presentation of the lectures that reads, "(commonly: 'object'—'subject'; actually: manifestness, understanding of being)" (Heidegger 2002a, 81). That is, as Dasein, we can have explicit truth, or untruth, only because the "soul" is understood as intrinsically relational (as Heidegger argues the Greeks understood it). We encounter entities in the world primarily as unconcealed from the background of tacit awareness, as manifest to us. To exist as Dasein is to exist in relation to Being, whether we are aware of it or not. Earlier in these lectures, he attributes to the "Theaetetus" the view that "the soul is itself a being-extended-to, a passage-way, an extending over to. It is the soul which, in its own relating of itself to something giveable, makes possible comportment towards" (Heidegger 2002a, 142; compare "*being held* out into the nothing" in "What is Metaphysics?" [Heidegger 1993, 103]).

This is how Heidegger reaches the position quoted in chapter 1: "These connections of being are not as such *conceived* and made into objects, but are *there* only in so far as they are reckoned with—how so? By perceiving and experiencing and dealing (and so forth) with beings" (Heidegger 2002a, 161). The technological "age of the world picture," by contrast, gives us a wrong, not to say perverse, understanding of truth as a representation that accurately reproduces an independent external reality. When God no longer serves as a universally acknowledged guarantor of the correctness of our beliefs in this Cartesian picture, as we have seen, modernity falls prey to more or less mitigated skepticism. Furthermore, we can see the manipulation of now decontextualized truths for the political and economic advantages of those with the power to fill the media with claims about global warming, evolution, and other matters that violate the dictates of science itself.

In effect, in these lectures and the earlier paper, "On the Essence of Truth," Heidegger has replaced temporality (which remains a metaphysical concept) with truth/alētheia as the key to understanding the being of Dasein. He has attempted to move beyond metaphysics not simply by reversing the positive and negative poles of the traditional metaphysical opposition, but also by embedding one in the other—the essence of truth is untruth—and then complicating the now "dominant" pole through the analysis of *pseudos* and its relationship to what is hidden/revealed in alētheia. And finally, he has shifted the discourse from the truth of beings to the Being of truth. Correlatively, Dasein is now not a being based in temporality, but is instead an openness oriented primarily toward comportment and secondarily toward beings as the beings they are (or are not). What is ordinarily understood by "truth" is, in turn, derived from that secondary kind of truth and ignores the truth of Being itself.

From these ideas, Heidegger's thought over the rest of his career moves in two main directions—backward toward the ancient Greeks and forward to the risk of the dominion of technology. These are not seen, however, as modes of temporality but, I would argue, as phases in a single narrative about how Dasein reveals or obscures Being itself. These lectures are centered on Plato, that is, on the history of philosophy, Heidegger reminds us, and "it is precisely *here*, and *only* here, in such *history*, that we experience the *presencing* of truth … above all by asking after *what* remained *un-happened* in this history and which was closed off, so much closed off that ever since it has seemed as if in its primordiality it *never was*" (Heidegger 2002a, 229; his emphasis).

III: Art, Truth, and Metaphysics

Before examining the texts that are considered to be clearly on the other side of the "*Kehre*"—the supposed dividing line between the earlier and later Heidegger—it might be helpful to briefly discuss another major paper from the early 1930s that addresses the question of truth and its relationship to Being, "The Origin of the Work of Art." The key question in this text is not how to get from truth to ontology, but how to get from art and aesthetics to ontology via truth.

Heidegger's initial move in this text is from work of art to thing, though he raises the possibility that "the work is at bottom something else and not a thing at all." He first separates out humans and animals (i.e., beings with souls, in Aristotle's terms) from "things." He then separates what remains into natural objects (including plants) and artifacts (Heidegger 1993, 146–47). After a slight detour through the history of philosophical accounts of what constitutes a thing—all of which he finds inadequate—he traces Aristotle's account in terms of form and matter back to equipment in the sense familiar from *Being and Time*. In equipment, or artifacts in general, some kind of raw material ("matter") is shaped ("form") for human use. What sets equipment apart from objects of nature and unites it with the work of art is that both are created by humans; what sets it apart from the work and unites the work with natural objects is that neither of these are made for human use (although natural objects obviously can be used by human once they exist, and indeed, one can also hang one's coat on an appropriately shaped statue). Equipment and natural objects are set apart from works of art in that the former items are, in the normal case, implicitly available as the things they are in our comportment with them. Works of art, by contrast, are what they are only when they are explicit objects of our attention (e.g., insofar as it is used as a coat rack, the statue fails to be a statue). Walking down the street, I am normally aware of my shoes only when I step on a patch of ice and find the soles are smooth enough to slide; I am normally aware of the snow bank next to me only when it becomes a preferable place to land compared to the pavement; and I am normally aware of the music in my ear buds except when keeping my balance overrides my engagement with it. Conversely, when all goes well, shoes (equipment) and snow bank (natural object) are there for me only implicitly, but music (art) is there explicitly (insofar as it is functioning as music and not as background for ruminating on the day ahead).

Heidegger's next rhetorical move is key—how do we come to understand the deeper meaning of the equipment that remains hidden while it supports our day-to-day comportment by helping to shape the openedness of things we encounter in that comportment? Heidegger answers this question, not by pointing to an actual piece of equipment, but by pointing to the famous Van Gogh painting of a pair of shoes. Heidegger states, "The artwork lets us know what shoes are in truth" (Heidegger 1993, 161). From this, he draws two conclusions. The first is that to look at the work of art as a kind of thing is to confuse its nature with the equipmentality of equipment. As viewed through the eyes of the technological age and, sadly, its educational system, it may be seen as purposeless equipment. The second conclusion is, "The artwork opens up in its own the Being of beings." That is, the work of art, by drawing attention to itself *as* art, also draws attention to the sphere of openedness from which it arose, the lighting or clearing which it illuminates and which illuminates it. Thus, the work of art reveals both truth and Being. Or, rather, since this might suggest a too significant role for the artist in that revealing and "it is precisely in great art—and only such art is under consideration here—that the artist remains inconsequential as compared with the work," one might say the truth of Being is revealed through art (Heidegger 1993, 164–66).

How does that happen? "[T]he work opens up a *world* and keeps it abidingly in force." This world, however, is not the immediate world of Dasein's caring found in *Being and Time*. This world is a larger one, the broader context within which our day-to-day comportment, our world of immediate concern, takes its meaning. Just as with "the nothing nothings" in the early translations of "What is Metaphysics," in this case, "The *world worlds*." This close relationship between this concept of world and the openedness of the clearing can be seen when Heidegger points out, in a passage we will return to in chapter 8, "A stone is worldless. Plant and animal likewise have no world; but they belong to the covert throng of a surrounding into which they are linked" (Heidegger 1993, 169–70; his emphasis). We have seen this division before—worldless, linked into a world ("besouled"), and with a world (having soul and discourse, which places things in that world). The work of art makes a world appear by revealing its own materiality, be it stone, oil paint, sound, or language. In so doing, it reveals the specific "strife" between world and earth and between human creation and that which resists it in the world from which the work arises: "*The work lets the earth be an earth*" (Heidegger 1993, 172; his emphasis). The work lets its material appear, not *as* material but as necessary to the existence of the work itself, in the same way that earth is necessary to the existence of a world. Paint became visible in paintings (e.g., in Van Gogh or Seurat) at the point in time when the ascendency of technology, which denies earth and refuses to acknowledge what resists it, made the materiality, the earth, of the painting important to how the work revealed the truths of its time.

Not only is this where this lecture articulates with Heidegger's critique of technology, it is also where it articulates with the discussions of truth. In returning to truth as alētheia, he states much more clearly than elsewhere that "it is not we who presuppose the unconcealment of beings; rather, the uncon-cealment of beings (Being) puts us in to such a condition of being that in our representation we always remain installed within and in attendance upon unconcealment." Truth (and falsity) are possible only because we are held out into the nothingness that allows things to exist for us as the things they are. But that nothing is not as total as the earlier formulations might suggest, if, for no other reason, than the *Angst* generated by such total nothingness would be unbearable. It is always—in the typical case, at least—mediated for us by a world of meanings. Those meanings are always partial, due to the presence in the world of an earth that resists full disclosure. For example, the Gothic cathe-dral meant to convey the total glory of God and perfect completeness of His world requires the flying buttresses and literal spandrels that are not counted as true parts of it. We have seen the same situation to be true with science and consciousness. For any particular thing to be true, "Not only must that *in con-formity* with which a cognition orders itself be already in some way unconcealed. The entire *realm* in which this 'conforming to something' goes on must already occur as a whole in the unconcealed; and this holds equally of that *for* which the conformity of a proposition to a matter becomes manifest." Think here again of the levels of truth previously discussed. A propositional truth is true only against a set of background assumptions, which can be made explicit if things go wrong enough, as in Kuhn. But that background relies on an even deeper layer of implicit truths, which only art, at its best, can reveal. Moreover, we as Dasein are knowers of truth only against this same background.

The nothing makes an unexpected (and often unnoted) reappearance here: "In the midst of beings as a whole an open place occurs. There is a clearing. Thought of in reference to beings, this clearing is more in being than are beings. This open center is therefore not surrounded by beings; rather, the clearing center itself encircles all that is, as does the nothing, which we scarcely know." All that exists for us, all that can be true (or false) for us is what is in that clearing. At the same time, "the center encircles" might be taken as an example of linguistic art in which Heidegger's efforts to reveal a truth about the human situation instead reveals the material limits of language. This is also the case with the great paradox of this lecture: "Truth, in its essence, is un-truth" (Heidegger 1993, 177–79; his emphasis). The essence of what is revealed, of "manifestness" (Heidegger 2002a, 18), is the unseen background that allows it to be revealed (or hidden) as what it is.

Great works of art free us, to some extent, from the "normal science" of our lives, so that we can see both the assumptions behind the normality and the possibility of other realities. "To submit to this displacement means to transform our accustomed ties to world and earth and henceforth to restrain all usual doing and prizing, knowing and looking, in order to say within the truth that is happening in the work" (Heidegger 1993, 191). One could say, for example, that Michelangelo's *Pietà* reorients our understanding of the humanity of Jesus by shifting the focus from his tortured body to his role as a son in relation to a mother, freeing us for a more psychological understanding of suffering. But note that this freeing is still tied to "the essential sacrifice" (Heidegger 1993, 187) at the core of Christianity. The truth in art comes from "the opening up of the open region, and the clearing of beings, [that] happens only when the openness that makes its advent in thrownness is projected" (i.e., when what is revealed in the human situation into which the artist is "thrown" appears in the work as part of its truth; in the case of Michelangelo, the religious beliefs of his time and place).

So far, we have examined art and truth. "*Art then is the becoming and happening of truth.*" But there is a paradox: "*All art ... is as such, in essence, poetry.*" Why is this? The answer is ontological—because "language alone brings beings as beings into the open for the first time. Where there is no language, as in the Being of stone, plant, animal, there is also no openness of beings, and consequently no openness of nonbeing and of the empty" (Heidegger 1993, 196–98; my interpolation). We are back to the earlier lectures on Aristotle. Our existence is as ensouled beings with discourse, as consciousnesses with language; we name things, categorize them, submit them to our will or let them be what they are in themselves. We can stand in the disclosedness of Being or we can hide in the darkness of Plato's Cave, absorbed in and tied to what appears to us without understanding the truth concealed behind it.

Notes

1. Interestingly, Geoffrey Bennington, the translator of Derrida's *The Beast and the Sovereign*, focused on *The Essence of Truth* in a plenary address on "The Politics of Politics (Heidegger, Derrida)" at the 2015 meeting of the Society for Phenomenology and Existential Philosophy. He presented an interesting counter to Derrida's critique of Heidegger on that basis. His address has since been published in *Scatter 1: The Politics of Politics in Foucault, Heidegger, and Derrida* (New York: Fordham Press, 2016), 93–101.

2. On epistemologies of ignorance, see Sullivan and Tuana, *Epistemologies of Ignorance*. On the relationship between epistemologies of ignorance and Heidegger, see the last chapter of *Ontological Humility*.

3. On this, see Ladelle McWhorter's brilliant *Racism and Sexual Oppression in Angle-America*.

4. This is another text in which the translator uses "being" where others and I would use "Being."

5. It is interesting that Plato, whose language does not give him the use/mention distinction that would enable him to differentiate sign, sense/concept, and referent, still provides the young Socrates with Theaetetus, a peer who shares his appearance (i.e., in part, his "referent"), and with a teacher who shares his sign or name (the older Socrates), so all the possible confusions are available.

6. Note again the similarity to American Pragmatism.

7. See chapter 3.

8. Again, the translator of this text does not capitalize "being," but I will do so when it appears outside of quotations in order to maintain consistency throughout my own text.

7 The Later Heidegger

Assuming [today's technological world] does not destroy itself.

—Martin Heidegger (*Identity and Difference*, 2002b, my interpolation)

I: *Parmenides*

Given Heidegger's tendency to label a lecture course as being on one subject but then talk primarily about a rather different subject, his lectures on ancient Greek philosophy address a range of topics. This is true of the 1942–43 lectures on *Parmenides*, which raise many of the same issues as *The Essence of Truth* from a decade earlier. Heidegger reminds us early in *Parmenides* that the ways in which we understand "truth" or "knowing" in the modern world are very different from the ways in which the ancient Greeks understood them. He does so in a manner familiar from his critique of technological modernity:

> What we usually call "knowing" is being acquainted with something and its qualities. In virtue of these cognitions we "master" things. This mastering "knowledge" is given over to a being at hand, to its structure and its usefulness. Such "knowledge" seizes the being, "dominates" it, and thereby goes beyond it and constantly surpasses it. The character of essential knowing is entirely different. It concerns the being in its ground—it intends Being…. [E]ssential knowing, heedfulness is a retreat in the face of Being. (Heidegger 1992, 4–5)

Because the ancient Greeks were closer to this essential knowing, or had not yet been lured away from it, "Anything resembling the self-certitude of the self-conscious subject is alien to the Greeks" (Heidegger 1992, 19). He makes it clear here, as elsewhere, that we cannot return to essential knowing in the way the Greeks experienced it: "For not only the essence of truth, but also the essence of everything essential, has in every case its own wealth, from which an age in history may only draw a small amount as its own portion" (Heidegger 1992, 11). His hope is always that we can find a way to move away from technology to draw our own "small amount" of the truth of our time.

In the discussion that follows these lectures about truth as correctness from Plato to Nietzsche, a familiar question arises from the focus on truth as the agreement between our statements or ideas and states of affairs in the external world: "How is it at all possible for an inner process of the mind or soul to be brought into agreement with the things out there?" In the move from Greek to Latin, Heidegger argues, alētheia disappears and is replaced with *veritas*. "*Veritas* as *rectitudo* is a quality of the mind or soul in the inner man." That is, truth loses both its social nature and its relationship to Being and belongs to "man," or the self or subject. In time, correctness becomes certitude and, within Christianity, the question arises regarding which individuals are "true" Christians, with justification and eventually justice in its wake. "The true, *verum*, is what is right, what vouches for certainty, and in that sense it is the righteous, the just." Even Nietzsche, Heidegger argues, falls into this way of thinking: "Everything 'anti' thinks in the spirit of that against which it is 'anti.'" For this reason, Western metaphysics reaches its peak in Nietzsche, and "The circle of the history of the essence of truth, as metaphysically experienced, in now closed. Yet ἀλήθεια remains outside this circle." Not only is it lost, "the field of the essence of ἀλήθεια is covered over with debris. But if that were all, then it would be an easy task to clear the debris and once again lay open this field. The difficulty is that it's not merely covered over with debris; there has been built on it an enormous bastion of the essence of truth determined in a manifold sense as 'Roman'" (Heidegger 1992, 50–53).

We can clearly see that, despite the title of these lectures, they are less an explication of an ancient Greek text than part of Heidegger's ongoing critique of technology as it has developed in post-Roman, Christian modernity. For example, his discussion of the goddess Ἀλήθεια in Parmenides' poem becomes an opportunity to address various levels of untruth as concealment.[1] One form of concealment is destruction: "What is no longer beside us, i.e., near-by... has disappeared, is absent; what is gone away is, in a certain sense, no more, it is destroyed." The United States, one might say, has "put aside" the role of slavery in its history and, hence, has not merely concealed it, but destroyed it, or tried to. In another kind of concealment, "the rare" "shelters and saves the concealed for what it is." If we take the Ark of the Covenant as an example of the rare, then "Raiders of the Lost Ark" would show what happens when we fail to save the rare "for what it is," because "the proper relation to the rare is not to chase after it but to leave it at rest by acknowledging the concealment."

Yet another form of concealment is the secret or mystery. Paradoxically, this is the concealment most readily found in the modern world, because the essence of the mystery "has been foreign to man from the moment he 'explained' the mysterious simply as the unexplained.... In this way the mysterious is only what is left over, what is not yet accounted for and incorporated within the circuit of explicative procedures."[2] For example, during my college days, the processes occurring in the "black box" of photosynthesis were a mystery, but now these precise processes are a commonplace of undergraduate biology. The clandestine and the inconspicuous are more obvious forms of concealment and can take the forms of camouflage and deception, bad science and bad faith. Finally, there is "the concealed in the sense of the merely not yet known" (Heidegger 1992, 61–63). All of these are forms of untruth as *pseudos*, which is not the opposite of alētheia, but relies, as we have seen, on a background of possible truth against which specific "truths" can become concealed.

For Heidegger, truth understood as disclosure and concealment, as opposed to correctness and representation, "is expressed in the word of the Greeks. It is what is said primordially" (Heidegger 1992, 67). Conversely, "'to have the word,' λόγον ἔχεν, is the essential characteristic of the humanity that became historical as Greek humanity." The Greeks understood themselves as living things set apart by their relationship with *logos*. Those peoples using different words, who sound as if they are only making noises like animals ("ba ba"), are not Greeks but "barbarians." By and large, the Greeks did not need to explicitly say this because it was simply their reality. However, "because the Greek essence of man is fulfilled in the 'to have the word,' Greek man could also 'have' and retain the word in that pre-eminent way we call silence" (Heidegger 1992, 78–79).

Through Pindar, Heidegger interprets *pragma* as meaning to travel along a path toward something and "on this way arrive at something and thereupon set it up as present." Here, *pragma* has not yet been sharply divided from *praxis* and "narrowed down to the concept of 'thing,' the matter 'at hand' to be dealt with, to be acted upon." Rather, "Things 'act' [*handeln*], insofar as the things present and at hand dwell within the reach of the hand."[3] Moreover, "Man does not 'have' hands, but the hand holds the essence of man, because the word as the essential realm of the hand is the ground of the essence of man." This primacy of the hand arises from the fact that "the hand exists as hand only where there is disclosure and concealment"—that is, we "handle" things (we act) where we have found answers to the questions we have placed regarding what is around us. This intersection of truth and action found in the word *pragma* clearly echoes the discussion in chapter 4 about being-underway in the lectures on "Sophist" (Heidegger 1992, 78–79).

Heidegger also states that *pragma* means "the still unseparated and essentially inseparable unity of the setting up in the arrival at something and of what is reached in the arrival and is then present as unconcealed" (Heidegger 1992, 80; translator's interpolation). Once again, we are "seeing beyond." The content of our experience is a result of what we bring to the situation and what we seek to find in it, as well as of what is "out there." Perception, deception, and perceptual error grow out of a searching for solutions to concrete problems that precedes the subject/object distinction. In one of Heidegger's favored examples, I do not cross a space full of explicitly perceived chairs to reach a lectern—rather, the classroom creates a situation in which any obstacle between the lectern and myself demands that I circumvent it to reach my goal.

While some American pragmatists might agree with this discussion up to this point, Heidegger emphasizes the impersonal or prepersonal nature of the perceptual situation, which is "originally experienced, not the grasping of something but the self-showing in view of which there first becomes possible a looking that grasps something." What is at issue here is more than intentionality, which he understands as "looking exclusively as man's representational self-direction toward beings" in an act of "re-presenting." By contrast, "The Greeks experience looking at first and properly as the way man emerges and comes into presence, *with* other beings" (Heidegger 1992, 103; my emphasis). A pragmatist might argue that what drives human knowing and perceiving is not an isolated subject, but the context in which it seeks to know and act in the world. Although Heidegger probably would not give that subject as much independent existence, he and the pragmatist might agree that the "functioning of the eyes does not give any information, and *cannot* give any information about the relation of man to beings. What is an 'eye' without the ability to see? We do not see *because* we have eyes, but we have eyes because we can 'see'" (Heidegger 1992, 146). In other words, we live and act in a world that poses visual questions to us, and we see in order to answer those questions.

In these lectures, Heidegger also offers an extended definition of the "epoch of modernity in the West":

> In this epoch, as a consequence of a peculiarly concealed incertitude, certitude in the sense of unconditional certainty counts as what is most valuable, and therefore ascertaining becomes the basic character of all comportment. Ascertaining is not merely subsequent corroboration but is rather the aggressive making secure in advance for the sake of certitude. The content and the reality of everything objective has whatever validity it has as the inexhaustible occasion for objectivization in the sense of the certification of the content of world and 'life.' Procedural processes (τέχνη) and their modes dominate experience. (Heidegger 1992, 128)

To understand precisely what he means here, one need only read Descartes's *Meditations*. Given this orientation toward the world, human existence takes a correlative form: "the essence of the Ego consists . . . in making every other being something stand over against it, its object, its over-and-against, its projected ob-ject." It, thus, becomes the epoch of subjectivity, "for only subjectivity marks off the essential bounds of an unconditioned objectivity and does so ultimately as a claim of its will."

Interestingly, given Heidegger's personal history and the dates of these lectures, he also states that only under these circumstances "do the concepts of 'nation' and 'people' obtain that metaphysical foundation from which they might possibly have historical relevance" (Heidegger 1992, 137). He adds, "The metaphysics lying at the foundation of the biologism of the nineteenth century and of psychoanalysis, namely the metaphysics of the complete oblivion of Being, is the source of an ignorance of all the laws of Being, the ultimate consequence of which is an uncanny hominization of the 'creature,' i.e., the animal, and a corresponding animalization of man" (Heidegger 1992, 152).[4] Because of this, "the mystery of the living being goes unheeded; for living beings are either exposed to the assault of chemistry or are transferred to the field of 'psychology.' Both presume to seek the riddle of life. They will never find it...because the riddle of life will never be found where the mystery of the living being has already been abandoned." (Heidegger 1992, 160). The question addressed more directly in his work on technology is how we might best answer the challenges presented to us by the modern age.

II: The Subject of Technology

As early in Heidegger's thinking on technology as "Modern Science, Mathematics, and Metaphysics" (1936), we discover the same description of science as a specific means of relating to "nature." In this paper, he makes a distinction between science in the early modern period, when "all scientists were philosophers" who "understood that there are no mere facts, but that a fact is only what it is in the light of the fundamental conception," and the positivism of his own era, which "thinks it can manage sufficiently with facts" and "concepts are merely expedients that one somehow needs, but should not get too involved with" (Heidegger 1993, 272). This paper begins with a comparison of contemporary understandings of mathematics and nature with the ancient Greek concepts of *ta mathēmata* and *physis*. If the latter topic seems all too familiar, Heidegger himself notes, "We steadfastly ask the *same* question—which in terms of utility is obviously useless." Here, the question concerns "The Difference Between the Greek Experience of Nature and That of Modern Times." To summarize, by Newton's time, "Nature is no longer the *inner* principle out of which the motion of the body follows; rather nature is the mode of the variety of the changing relative positions of bodies, the manner in which they are present in space and time, which themselves are domains of possible positional orders and determinations of order and have no special traits anywhere." In contrast to the usual claim about the empirical basis of modern science versus the abstract reasoning of Aristotle and the other ancients, Heidegger notes that Newton's first law of motion (the law of inertia) describes the motion of a body "left to itself," without contact with any other entity or force—that is, "a thing that does not exist." Rather than being based on observation, the law of inertia "demands a fundamental representation of things that contradict the ordinary" (Heidegger 1993, 288–90).

Heidegger finds the hallmark of modern science not in its method, but in the fact that it envisions nature as "the realm of uniform space-time context of motion," which "makes possible and requires a universal uniform measure as an essential determinant of things, i.e., numerical measurement" (Heidegger 1992, 292–93). He lays responsibility for "the mathematical foundation of modern Dasein" not, as usual, at the door of the Romans—he explicitly excludes the role of Christianity (Heidegger 1993, 298)—but at the doors of the French, English, and Dutch, even to the point of emphasizing the four years Leibniz spent in Paris (Heidegger 1993, 296–97).[5] This may be because his primary focus, besides Newton, is Descartes, whom he considers the source of modern philosophy as defined by a focus on the mathematical and by the mind/body dichotomy.

Since Heidegger believes that "procedure, i.e., how in general we are to pursue things (*methodos*), decides in advance what truth we shall seek out in the things," the method laid out in Descartes's "Rules for the Direction of the Mind" results in a specific logic.[6] Our axioms, or basic knowledge, must be certain and "establish in advance…what is in being and what Being means" so we can know what a thing is. This means that "all knowledge up to now must necessarily be put into question," thereby cutting us off from the everyday pragmatic concerns that led us to adopt this method in the first place, as well as from our history. For such a method to work, all knowledge must take the form of a proposition, a proposition accompanied by an "I think," thus tying together the technological concepts of knowledge and ourselves. On this reading, for Descartes, "The Being of beings is determined out of the 'I think'." So we never investigate the "ego" except as the subject of the "I think," allowing the subject to shift between the "subject" that knows and the "subject" known (Heidegger 1993, 300–304). From here starts our slow slide toward becoming part of the "standing reserve" as envisioned in "The Question Concerning Technology."

Heidegger makes clear in "The Age of the World Picture" (1938) that each age has its own way to make sense of the beings it encounters and to find answers to the questions that arise from these encounters.[7] For this reason, "it makes no sense whatever to suppose that modern science is more exact than that of antiquity.… No one would presume to say that Shakespeare's poetry is more advanced than that of Aeschylus" (Heidegger 1977, 117).[8] Since we encounter things only in the context of an already meaningful social world, there is no one standard of correctness or exactness in our relationship to nature. It is what we seek to know that shapes what is real for us, not the other way around. He continues to focus on the mathematical that is characteristic of Western modernity and on "mathematical research into nature"—that is, science as a whole. This approach to nature is not "exact because it calculates with precision; rather it must calculate in this way because its adherence to its object-sphere has the character of exactitude" and its subject, nature, must be such that it can be measured exactly. Thus, "physical science does not first become research through experiment; rather, on the contrary, experiment first becomes possible where and only where the knowledge of nature has been transformed into research" (Heidegger 1977, 119–21).

As we saw in Heidegger's lectures during an earlier war, his comments on the relative importance of science carry a subtext tied to the politics of the university. Again in 1938, he asks, "What is taking place in this extending and consolidating of the institutional character of the sciences? Nothing less than the making secure of the precedence of methodology over whatever is…. The scholar disappears. He is succeeded by the research man who is engaged in research projects" (Heidegger 1977, 125). Under this regime, "Nature and history become the objects of a representing that explains. Such representing counts on nature and takes account of history. Only that which becomes object in this way *is*—is considered to be in being" (Heidegger 1977, 127; his emphasis).

Correlative to this "objectiveness" of things stands, as we have previously seen, a specific understanding of what we as "subjects" are—an understanding that Heidegger traces once again to Descartes's subject/object dyad. He admits that modern Dasein has freed himself [sic] "from the bonds of the Middle Ages in freeing himself to himself" and introduced "subjectivism and individualism. But it remains just as certain that no age before this one has produced a comparable objectivism and that in no age before this has the non-individual, in the form of the collective, come to acceptance as having worth."[9] In becoming *"subiectum,"* Heidegger argues, "Man becomes that being upon which all that is, is grounded as regards the manner of its Being and its truth." It is no longer the case that things can be the things that they are only for a consciousness that can take them as such, nor that their truth can only be a truth for a being capable of both truth and deception. Both of those claims are fully compatible with beings and their truth being given to Dasein by Being, which remains in both its ancient and medieval forms a recognizable, if irreducible and ultimately unknowable, mystery. In the modern age, Being, understood as God or the gods, has disappeared, and "man becomes the relational center of that which is as such" (Heidegger 1977, 127–28).

Our world is not an open space of meaning in which we encounter objects of use that point beyond themselves to an understanding of the deeper meaning of our lives and of Being. Rather, thanks to Descartes and others, our world is a representation in which everything is exposed as simply what it is and no more—an object of study that we contemplate from afar. "Where the world becomes picture, what is, in its entirety, is juxtaposed as that for which man is prepared and which, correspondingly, he therefore intends to bring before himself" (Heidegger 1977, 129). Dasein, not Being, has become the center and the source. This is why *Being and Time* is both pivotal and problematic. As Beaufret notes, the *Kehre* shifts Heidegger's focus from Dasein to Being itself.

Heidegger goes on to say, "It is no wonder that humanism first arises where the world becomes picture" because humanism "designates the philosophical interpretation of man which explains and evaluates whatever is, in its entirety, from the standpoint of man and in relation to man" (Heidegger 1977, 133). This explains his wariness of the expression "human being." If the world is picture, humans are the observers and judges of what is in that picture, and whatever is outside of that picture, outside the scope of our vision ceases to exist. In the appendices to "The Age of the World Picture," he contrasts this humanistic understanding of Dasein to what he sees as Plato's concept of the self in "Theaetetus":[10] "Through man's being limited to that which, at any particular time, is unconcealed, there is given to him the measure that always confines a self to this or that. Man does not [for Plato], from out of some detached I-ness, set forth the measure to which everything that is, in its Being, must accommodate itself" (Heidegger 1977, 145–46; my interpolation). For the ancient Greeks, man "cannot become *subiectum* because here Being is presencing and truth is unconcealment" (Heidegger 1977, 147). From this idea arises one of the most powerful and visionary statements of those Heidegger suppressed when he presented this paper:

> In the planetary imperialism of technologically organized man, the subjectivism of man attains its acme, from which point it will descend to the level of organized uniformity and there firmly establish itself. This uniformity becomes the surest instrument of total, i.e., technological, rule over the earth. The modern freedom of subjectivity vanishes totally in the objectivity commensurate with it. Man cannot, of himself, abandon this destining of his modern essence or abolish it by fiat. But man can, as he thinks ahead, ponder this: Being subject as humanity has not always been the sole possibility belonging to the essence of historical man, which is always beginning in a primal way, nor will it always be. (Heidegger 1977, 152–53)

Here lies the link between his work on the Greek and his critique of the modern age.

In 1955, long before smartphones, Heidegger notes in "The Question Concerning Technology" that modern Dasein is "chained to technology, whether we passionately affirm or deny it. But we are delivered over to it in the worst possible way when we regard it as something neutral." For Heidegger, technology has some of the character of a world-defining work of art—it shapes our world in such a way that we cannot escape by mere denial or by a flight into the semblance of an earlier age. Given this, it would seem as if "everything depends on our manipulating technology in the proper manner.... The will to mastery becomes all the more urgent the more technology threatens to slip from human control" (Heidegger 1977, 4–5).

To disclose or uncover the truth about modern technology, he contrasts it with the ancient Greek technē based on Aristotle's four causes—a "bringing-forth" through which "the growing things of nature as well as whatever is completed through the crafts and arts come at any given time to their appearance.... This coming rests and moves freely within what we call revealing [*das Engbergen*]. The Greeks have the word *alētheia* for revealing" (Heidegger 1977, 11–12; translator's interpolation). He then repositions the significance of science: "It is said that modern technology is something incomparably different from all earlier technologies because it is based on modern physics as an exact science. Meanwhile, we have come to understand more clearly that the reverse holds true as well: Modern physics, as experimental, is dependent upon technical apparatus and upon progress in the building of apparatus." Thus, technology too, is a revealing, but one that "challenges" nature, reducing the four causes to the purely "efficient" production of vast quantities of things and the energy required to make more of them (Heidegger 1977, 14). The paradigmatic "work of art" is no longer the Greek temple or the medieval cathedral, but the "airliner that stands on the runway" (Heidegger 1977, 17).

Heidegger recounts the history of modern science in somewhat shorter form than in 1936, invoking the concept of "enframing" from "The Age of the World Picture." Then, he returns to the correlate of this new form of "objectivism"—the new "subjectivism" of modern Dasein, specifically the "freedom" that was central to the existentialists' concept of the human situation. That they are his tacit target is clear when he begins, "The essence of freedom is *originally* not connected with the will or even with the causality of human willing." Rather, freedom belongs primarily to what is revealed, the happening of truth, "but that which frees—the mystery—is concealed and always concealing itself." As the translator points out in a footnote, Heidegger's point here is clearer in German, where *die Freiheit* carries the echo of *das Freie*, the word he uses here for the "open," or what he calls elsewhere the "clearing." This point underscores the association he wants to make between freedom and the open space in which Dasein exists and acts, so that only in a secondary sense is freedom attributed to those actions.

This consideration regarding freedom is significant for two reasons. One is that even this secondary freedom allows Dasein to do more than "push blindly on with technology or, what comes to the same thing, to rebel helplessly against it." If we understand technology for what it is in its essence, "we find ourselves unexpectedly taken into a freeing claim." But we are freed by recognizing the other reason that freedom is important here. The gravest danger of technology is not nuclear annihilation, but the fact that the enframing of technology has the potential, as we will see, to cut off Dasein's access to any open other than the open created by technology itself: "man, thus under way, is continually approaching the brink of the possibility of pursuing and pushing forward nothing but what is revealed in ordering, and of deriving all his standards on this basis" (Heidegger 1977, 25–26; his emphasis).

That is, the danger of technology is precisely an answer, perhaps the most natural and likely answer, to the question Heidegger asked in 1919—"*What is the psychic*?" The true threat is not "psychologism" as a philosophical error or the ascendency of the sciences in the university, but the fact that technology has the power, if left unchecked, to reduce our understanding of ourselves to what can be measured and counted by psychology and the other social sciences. This is ultimately what transforms us into "subjects" in all senses of the term—as agents, as objects of political power, and as objects of study—with no clear division or distinction between the three types of subject.[11] Technology denies our primary existence as questioners and interpreters of the "*Umwelt*." Thus, it opens the possibility of not only becoming mere organic cogs in the technological machine, but also of no longer being able to envision other interpretations of our existence.[12] The technological age "threatens man with the possibility that it could be denied to him to enter into a more original revealing and hence to experience the call of a more primordial truth" about both nature and ourselves (Heidegger 1977, 28).[13] This threat is why "questioning is the piety of thought" (Heidegger 1977, 35). With its call to the arts in general, and poetry in particular, as the source of a possible alternative to the technological age, "The Question Concerning Technology" begins the transition in Heidegger's later work from countering the pull of technology by argument to the invocation of poetry and, after 1964, to the same silence he noted in the ancient Greeks.

III: The Last Heidegger

In addition to his lectures on the ancient Greeks and his critique of modern technology, Heidegger presented several papers on other topics in the 1950s and 1960s, and we have summaries or transcripts of some of his seminars into the 1970s. In many of these texts, the themes we have been following in his work since 1919 continue to reappear. In "The Principle of Identity" (1957), for example, he again sketches out the basic paradox that underlies modern science: "if science could not be sure in advance of the identity of its object in each case, it would not be what it is. By this assurance, research makes certain that its work is possible. Still, the leading idea of the identity of the object is never of any palpable use to the sciences. Thus, what is successful and fruitful about scientific knowledge is everywhere based on something useless." As in the 1919 lectures, he uses the image of a leap or spring (*Sprung* in both texts) to describe the move we need to make to escape the downward spiral of Western modernity. What he calls a "moving away from the attitude of representational thinking" is a leap/spring that "leaps away, away from the habitual ideas of man as the rational animal who in modern times has become a subject for his objects. Simultaneously, the spring also leaps away from Being. But Being, since the beginning of Western thought, has been interpreted as the ground in which every being as such is grounded." It is important to note here that this is not a leap away from Being *per se*, but a leap away from Being as understood in Western metaphysics. "Where does the spring go that springs away from the ground? Into an abyss? Yes, as long as we only represent the spring in the horizon of metaphysical thinking. No, insofar as we spring and let go. Where to? To where we already have access: the belonging to Being. Being itself, however, belongs to us; for only with us can Being be present as Being, that is, become present."

He explains this leap away in terms of technology, which governs the "habitual ideas" in "modern times." Invoking the term "atomic age," he says that we can experience "how Being becomes present to us today in the world of technology. But may we simply equate the world of technology with Being? Obviously not." The problem, as we have seen through the course of his thinking, is that in the modern age "the above-mentioned totality of the world of technology is interpreted in advance in terms of man, as being of man's making" (Heidegger 2002b, 32–34). He then recapitulates much of the argument of "The Question Concerning Technology," but he uses a new vocabulary centered on the concept of *Ereignis* (literally, "event").[14] He returns at the end of this article, however, to where we started, with the concept of "nature": "But what authority has decided that nature as such must forever *remain* the nature of modern physics...? We cannot, of course, reject today's technological world as [the] devil's work, nor may we destroy [*vernichten*, annihilate] it—assuming it does not destroy itself" (Heidegger 2002b, 40; my interpolations). But a greater danger than nuclear war, as we already saw, is the loss of the possibility of the "spring" across the "abyss" to a new relationship with Being. In "Time and Being" (1962), which returns to the concept of the "*es gibt*" from *Being and Time*, he writes, "If man were not the constant receiver of the gift given by the 'It gives presence,' if that which is extended in the gift did not reach man, then not only would Being remain concealed in the absence of this gift, not only closed off, but man would remain excluded from the scope of: It gives Being. Man would not be man" (Heidegger 1972, 12).

In an echo of the discussion of artificial intelligence in chapter 2, the text of "The End of Philosophy and the Task of Thinking" (1964) notes a shift in modernity from science to "cybernetics," which "transforms language into an exchange of news. The arts become regulated-regulating instruments of information" (Heidegger 1972, 58). Yet Heidegger remains hopeful that "the world civilization which is just now beginning might one day overcome the technological-scientific-industrial [!] character as the sole criterion of man's world sojourn" (Heidegger 1972, 60; my interpolation). He returns to the motto of phenomenology, "to the things themselves," and notes that for Husserl this means "what is at stake in the philosophical investigation" is "the subjectivity of consciousness." That is, phenomenology remains squarely within metaphysics: "The matter of philosophy as metaphysics is the Being of beings, their presence in the form of substantiality and subjectivity" (Heidegger 1972, 62).

For Heidegger, the more important question is "what remains unthought in the matter of philosophy?" (Heidegger 1972, 64), His answer is what he now calls "the opening," a concept we have seen before as "the open space" and "the clearing." The opening "is spoken about in philosophy's beginning. How does this occur and with which names?" The answer, of course, lies in Parmenides' invocation of the goddess *Alētheia*. "We must think *alētheia*, unconcealment, as the opening which first grants Being and thinking and their presencing to and for each other" (Heidegger 1972, 67–68). Thus, we see the centrality of his work on "the essence of truth" in the 1930s for his thinking as a whole, although now he says that, "To raise the question of *alētheia*, of unconcealment as such, is not the same as raising the question of truth." The reduction of unconcealment to "correctness and dependability," he suggests, is a product of Dasein's focus on what is present for it, what is "given" to it as concealed. "Does this happen by chance?" he asks. "Or does it happen because self-concealing, concealment, *lēthe*, belongs to *a-lētheia*" at its heart? "If this were so, then with these questions we would reach the path to the task of thinking at the end of philosophy." (Heidegger 1972, 71).

"The End of Philosophy and the Task of Thinking" was Heidegger's last published work, but he did not entirely abandon the themes under discussion here; the seminars he taught from 1966 to 1973 reflect the same preoccupations. A relatively direct (and familiar) account of the development of modern concepts of subjectivity and nature in the 1968 seminar begins with a bold claim: "What is in fact the driving force of the subject-object dichotomy? It is the quest for absolute certainty." He further claims that "the quest for certainty appears first in the domain of faith... (Luther), then in the domain of physics as the search for the *mathematical* certainty of nature (Galileo)."[15] The question becomes, "How is it possible to grasp in one concept, with a compelling necessity, the unity of mathematical certainty and the certainty of salvation?" The answer is found in Descartes's subject-object dualism. This dichotomy creates inner certainty and externalizes doubt to nature, which is emptied of all meaning. For Heidegger, "What is decisive is that the subject-object distinction plays out entirely in the dimension of subjectivity" (Heidegger 2003, 13–14; his emphasis). However, subjectivity cannot become an object for science because "the autopsy of a brain does not reveal any 'representations'" (Heidegger 2003, 31).

He continues with this theme to ask of the Louvre—as he did of the Feldberg Tower in *The Essence of Truth* (Heidegger 2002a, 210–15)—what it is that we represent to ourselves when we think of the great museum. Is it an image of the Louvre or the Louvre itself? The obvious answer is the Louvre itself.[16] Perception works in the same way—that is, we see the Louvre, but with the added element that it is present to my body in a way in which it is not when I think of it or remember it. What is this body? It is my "lived-body," which he characterizes as "something like the reach of the human body," for which "last night, the moon was closer than the Louvre" because it was in the immediate perceived field. The lived-body, as we saw with the Aristotelian psyché, is not the biological body. It is neither mind nor external nature, but the condition of the possibility of both. "The limit of the body is the skin. The limit of the 'lived-body' is more difficult to determine. It is not 'world' but it is perhaps just as little 'environment'" (Heidegger 2003, 31–32). The "biological body," as a part of nature or as opposed to it, exists only for the modern subject that was born at the same time.

In these seminars, Heidegger also returns to the concept of "opposedness" as the common source of mind and nature. He begins by reaffirming the distance between his work and the usual concept of intentionality: "*Being and Time* no long speaks of consciousness.... For Husserl this was a pure scandal!" He then relates consciousness to the German *Wissen* (knowing),[17] which, in turn, is related to the Latin *videre* (to see) "in the sense that knowing is having-seen." Next, he asks, "What is the basis of this having-seen for any consciousness? The fundamental possibility for the human being to traverse an open expanse in order to reach things." What gives us knowledge and what allows us to "have-seen" is not the intentionality of a Cartesian ego, but the open space of opposedness, the realm of beings as a whole in which we "reckon with" the objects of our everyday concern as beings embodied and embedded in a world we encounter as already shared and meaningful. The account of the seminar goes on to note, "This being-in-the-open-expanse is what *Being and Time* called (Heidegger adds: 'very awkwardly and in an unhelpful way') Dasein" (Heidegger 2003, 68–69; recorder's interpolation).

Thus, all the themes we have been following in Heidegger's work come together here. Dasein, or whatever "awkward and unhelpful" term we might use to describe human existence, moves from its immediate day-to-day preoccupations to an ever larger social and natural world while remaining ignorant of beings as a whole and, hence, of Being. In the European tradition, that world has evolved into one in which the science of nature is allowed, if not required, to define consciousness, or Dasein itself. As a "mind" reduced to the same scientific—that is, technological—terms as the "body" it animates, as part of nature, Dasein becomes one more "thing" explained in terms of mass and motion. This technological view of what we are denies and puts at risk what has always been the core of existence for Heidegger—our nature as an entity "distinguished by the fact that, in its very Being, that Being is an *issue* for it" (Heidegger 1962, 32; his emphasis).

Notes

1. This discussion bears comparison with recent discourse on "epistemologies of ignorance." On this, see Sullivan and Tuana, *Race and Epistemologies of Ignorance*, as well as Holland, *Ontological Humility*.

2. It is helpful to keep the religious meaning of "mystery" in mind, rather than mystery novels.

3. We will return to the role of the hand in Heidegger's thought in chapter 8.

4. We will also return to this topic in chapter 8.

5. One could speculate on reasons for this, given the date of this lecture.

6. Compare Thomas Kuhn, *The Structure of Scientific Revolutions*.

7. In reading this section it is helpful to keep in mind Michel Foucault's discussion of Diego Velázquez's *Las Meninas* and, indeed, all of *The Order of Things* (Foucault 1970, 3–16).

8. I cannot let pass without comment the reference to Shakespeare as the equal of Aeschylus in 1938, rather than, say, Hölderlin—especially considering that about half the text of this lecture was suppressed at the time of its original presentation (Heidegger 1972, x)

9. Again, I must note the 1938 publication date and point out that, although the reference to the "collective" could be read as a criticism of communism, the Nazis also represented themselves as "socialists."

10. This is based on a reading of Socrates' famous paraphrase of Protagoras at 152 (a), usually translated as "Man is the measure of all things."

11. This is another point at which Heidegger's work articulates with Foucault's thought.

12. With regard to the former possibility, one is reminded of "Frontios," an episode from the twenty-first season of *Dr. Who* in which disembodied human brains are used to run a machine called the "Tractator" (!) in the service of an alien civilization. In a less light-hearted vein, one might consider the attitude of Apartheid-era South Africa toward its indigenous population (see Jacques Derrida's "Racism's Last Word") or that of the Nazi regime toward the Poles and other Slavic peoples of Eastern Europe.

13. Cf. contemporary political moves to defund arts education in the public schools, and the current devaluation of the humanities and the arts in higher education in favor of the sciences and other more "practical" disciplines.

14. For a fuller discussion of Heidegger's etymology for this term and its role in his thought, see Holland, *The Madwoman's Reason* (1998).

15. Compare the similar discussion of Newton and Galileo in "Modern Science, Metaphysics, and Mathematics" (1936) (Heidegger 1993, 271–305).

16. The politically interesting shift from the tower in the Black Forest to the center of French culture was made, perhaps, in deference to his hosts in Le Thor.

17. But note also that "science" is "*Wissenschaft*" (roughly, the production of knowledge).

8 Reading Heidegger After Heidegger

> There is not and there could not be and there must not be any inheritance or filiation worthy of these appellations without transformation, re-beginning, re-invention, diverting, resistance, rebellions, and sometimes also betrayal—and especially without an interbreeding of genealogies.
>
> —Jacques Derrida (*On Touching—Jean-Luc Nancy*, 2005)

I: Heidegger and a World of Absorbed Copers

Much of what I would want to say about Hubert Dreyfus's interpretations of Heidegger is summed up in the fact that his two most famous books are *What Computers Can't Do* and *Being-in-the-World: A Commentary on Heidegger's "Being and Time," Division I*. The latter text remains the definitive study of *Being and Time* in English (and, I would wager, any other language), and its influence on my thought should be apparent throughout the present book. Here, I will discuss that text briefly to find more resonances between Dreyfus's interpretation and my own, then go on to suggest why it appears that the corner of the academic world in which Dreyfus found himself may have diverted him from developing an understanding of Heidegger's later work that could match the depth and power of his interpretation of *Being and Time*.

Given the focus of the present book, it might make sense to begin with the section of *Being-in-the-World* on "Heidegger's Critique of Recent Versions of Cartesianism." Dreyfus explains that, for Heidegger, "Natural science tells us how hammers work but not what hammers *are*. It does not have to account for the being of equipment such as hammers, but only for the causal powers of the natural kinds of materials such as iron and wood out of which hammers are made" (Dreyfus 1991, 113). As we have previously seen, hammers are hammers only within a world that makes sense of hammering. Otherwise, they are just awkward, heavy lumps of wood and metal. Thus, the hammer-in-use is ontologically prior to the hammer-for-science. Dreyfus then follows Heidegger in noting that traditional philosophy, in trying to build meaning and "values" back into the world as seen by science, fails because "objectivity" requires that scientists strip entities of their meaning before they can even start to study them. This suggests, as I noted at the beginning of this book, that "science has a legitimate place in explaining the equipmental whole." Science reveals what was already present-but-hidden (though those are not Dreyfus's terms) in our everyday encounters with things, but "it discovers the physical properties of nature by leaving out all relevance to human purposes" (Dreyfus 1991, 120–21). The interesting *philosophical* question is an ontological one about the being of beings and, more importantly in *Being and Time*, the being of Dasein.

More relevant to our discussion here, Dreyfus makes a clear distinction between Heidegger's thought and intentionality as normally understood, most notably by Husserl and Sartre. For Heidegger, "Dasein must be understood to be more basic than mental states and their intentionality." Dreyfus explains this in terms of Dasein's nature as self-interpreting, which he calls "existence." Existence, in this sense, is prior to consciousness in that, as we saw in the counter-case of traditional zombies, we have to want something and to have goals embedded in a meaningful world in order to exist as human at all. We interpret ourselves as beings or people of a certain sort and, on that basis, we act in the world. Dreyfus's main concern in this section is to explain that Dasein can be either a singular or a collective concept, both I-Dasein and we-Dasein, which he emphasizes to combat the individualism of Sartre's account. It is perhaps telling, however, that Dreyfus himself chooses the term "human being" to capture the I/we-ness of Dasein, despite the warnings about that term in Heidegger's "Letter on Humanism" and elsewhere (Dreyfus 1991, 13–15). For Heidegger, the term "human" carries with it an entire metaphysics that he sought to avoid because "is the damage caused by all such terms still not sufficiently obvious?" (Heidegger 1993, 219). The use of everyday language in which to explain Heidegger, which otherwise generally serves Dreyfus well, also becomes problematic in his reliance on a concept of "culture" that runs the risks inherent in that word as pointed out by Heidegger in *Introduction to Metaphysics* (Heidegger 2000, 50–51).

Later in *Being-in-the-World*, Dreyfus returns to Heidegger's critique of intentionality in a way that reveals how radical Heidegger's thinking truly is, including how different it is from Husserl's thought and from American pragmatism. Dreyfus argues that Heidegger does more than reverse the usual priority of disinterested thought over action in philosophical discourse. He also shows that "neither practical activity nor contemplative knowledge can be understood as a relation between a self-sufficient mind and an independent world" (Dreyfus 1991, 49). Implicit in this perspective is the observation that "the whole idea of transcending from the inner to the outer must be revised." Dreyfus points to Heidegger's use of "comportment" (*Verhalten*, a term used as early as *Toward the Definition of Philosophy*, in 1919) to solve this problem, "because the term has no mentalistic overtones." Dreyfus also notes that, for Heidegger, "the whole machinery of the mental is a construction of the theorist."

At the same time, Dreyfus suggests that Heidegger's account of intentionality, which he terms "the fundamental point of Division One of *Being and Time*," required clarification and augmentation in later lectures and is paradoxically complete only in *Basic Problems of Phenomenology*, in which "Heidegger's rejection of *all* purely mentalistic forms of intentionality is fully explicit" (Dreyfus 1991, 51–54). Dreyfus twice refers to Heidegger's acknowledgment that the body has its own problematic (Heidegger 1962, 143; cited at Dreyfus 1991, 41, 137), but he points out that, for Heidegger, bodily spatiality is measured in terms of "accessibility," not literal distances, as we saw in *Four Seminars*, so "a thing is near to me when I can get a maximal grip on it" (Dreyfus 1991, 133). Ease of access also explains how Heidegger understands the left/right orientation of human interaction with the material world without making the physical body itself an essential aspect of our being, a solution Dreyfus describes as "consistent, but ... unsatisfying" (Dreyfus 1991, 137).

The general outline of my argument about the understanding of consciousness and the mind/body problem in Heidegger is, thus, already apparent in Dreyfus's text, but it remains just that—an outline. Rather than expand his interpretation into a more general re-evaluation of the importance of Heidegger's thought for philosophy (and the sciences), Dreyfus's work after *Being-in-the-World* tends to focus primarily on two narrower projects. These are the argument against artificial intelligence, which he had begun from a largely Merleau-Pontyan perspective in *What Computers Can't Do*, and the ongoing engagement with the work of Michel Foucault, John Searle, and others, where Dreyfus's arguments are often based on Heidegger's thought but do not address it directly. A 2006 article titled "Overcoming the Myth of the Mental," for example, does not engage with the texts discussed above that suggest a deeply radical strain in Heidegger that would deny and undermine the entire mental/physical split and the metaphysics it entails. Rather, it remains focused on, as the abstract states, "how philosophers who want to understand knowledge and action can profit from a phenomenological analysis of the nonconceptual embodied coping skills we share with animals and infants" (Dreyfus 2006, 43). One could argue that, in reaction to Sartre's individualistic and voluntaristic readings of *Being and Time*, Dreyfus focuses too narrowly on the social and on "absorbed coping," and so retains the basic structure of traditional metaphysics rather than undoing that structure. Or, one could argue that, while he avoids the Germanic-American "piety" and French "irreverence" cited in chapter 1, Dreyfus might err by turning his attention to the sciences and social sciences rather than away from them, as Heidegger would urge us to do.

II: Heidegger With and Without Being

Since I have limited my discussion largely to Heidegger's critical stance toward the philosophical tradition, especially with regard to consciousness, I turn in this section to two recent attempts to offer a comprehensive and unified interpretation of Heidegger's "positive" account of "fundamental ontology." I will discuss Thomas Sheehan's *Making Sense of Heidegger* and, more briefly, Richard Capobianco's *Heidegger's Way of Being* as representatives of the two generally opposite directions in contemporary efforts to move outside the "box" of traditional Heidegger scholarship. Unfortunately, I would argue, neither side has yet captured the "new wave" of thought on his work.[1]

Capobianco explains the contrast between his interpretation and those of both Dreyfus and Sheehan in a footnote: "Sheehan and Dreyfus read Heidegger from within very different philosophical traditions, no doubt, but it remains, nonetheless, that for both the central matter of Heidegger's thinking concerns the human being—Dasein and Dasein's making 'sense' of things" (Capobianco 2014, 101). Capobianco's view is that Being is "the fundamental matter of Heidegger's lifetime of thinking." While drawing from many of the same texts as I do, he argues that the recent move toward relating Heidegger's thoughts to "all sorts of practical social, political, environmental, and design concerns," which "yielded interesting and even helpful results," has all the same left the matter of Being "almost entirely behind' (Capobianco 2014, 3). He offers an interpretation of Heidegger that he believes returns Being to its proper place at the center of his thought, though he notes, "This by no means diminishes the human being, not at all. It is simply to recognize the *limit* of our marvelous *logos*, our comprehensibility (*Verstehbarkeit*), our taking-as, our meaning-making. Manifestation [by physis, which he equates with Being] structurally precedes and exceeds any kind and any level of meaning" (Capobianco 2014, 63). He argues that readings such as Dreyfus's and Sheehan's "perpetuate the very 'forgottenness' of Being that Heidegger so often lamented," and such readings represent "a falling back into the 'subjectivism' of the modern philosophy of consciousness and language that he strove so hard to overcome" (Capobianco 2014, 68). This suggests a clearer account of how Heidegger understands consciousness is central to this debate. I have attempted to reconcile the question of priority between Being and Dasein by finding in Heidegger's text an account that redefines consciousness in such a way that it is always intrinsically and necessarily linked to Being. This would allow us to both honor Heidegger's own commitment to the primacy of Being and to make use of the resources his thinking provides for solving the problems of the present age. The main point on which Capobianco and I generally agree is that "Heidegger seemed to have become especially frustrated that his earlier formulations were still not understood in the proper way" (Capobianco 2014, 39).

Sheehan, on the other hand, states at the beginning of *Making Sense of Heidegger* that he understands his work as "not about 'being' as Western philosophy has understood that term for over twenty-five hundred years, but rather about sense itself: meaningfulness and its source" (Sheehan 2015, xi). In general, he seems to concur with my interpretation of Heidegger on the question of consciousness. For example, he draws on his exhaustive knowledge of Heidegger's

Gesamtausgabe to argue with regard to things that "their appearance as knowable and usable, occurs only in an actual encounter with a human being. In fact, the disclosedness of a thing does not belong to the *thing* but to *ex-sistence*." Sheehan then links this thought to the previously made point about Aristotle to distinguish between a "sentient disclosedness of things" and "meaningful presence insofar as [human beings] take the thing (correctly or incorrectly) *as* something or other" (Sheehan 2015, 80; my interpolation). Thus, "For Heidegger, 'being' refers not to the mere physical presence of a thing to the sense organs. Rather, it refers to the meaningful presence of things, which is given only with human beings" (Sheehan 2015, 112; but see also, e.g., 146). Although Sheehan uses the term "human being," which Heidegger rejects, he generally avoids the "humanism" that Sartre falls into. Sheehan retranslates a passage from *Being and Time* (Heidegger 1962, 415) to emphasize the limits of human control: "The fact that such things get dis-covered along with the openedness of our own ex-sistence does not mean that this matter is under our control. Only *what*, in *which* direction, *to what extent and how* we actually dis-cover and dis-close is a matter of our freedom, although always within the limits of our thrownness" (Sheehan 2015, 206, his emphasis).

Sheehan's argument is, of course, a much broader one than mine. To summarize much too briefly, his basic point is that Heidegger's main insight consisted of the realization that "the thrown-openness of ex-sistence, can never come into the open (a fact the Heidegger called *Ent-eignis*) precisely because it is the necessarily presupposed reason why there is an open at all" (Sheehan 2015, 78). In support of this argument, Sheehan redefines *Sein* in Heidegger as "the meaningfulness of things," adding that Heidegger "wanted to move beyond this meaningfulness to what makes it possible," and he found this in "the 'realm of disclosedness or clearing (intelligibility)'" (Sheehan 2015, 189–90). Sheehan also sees *Entschlossenheit* (usually translated as "resoluteness") as the primary moral virtue in Heidegger (see, e.g., Sheehan 2015, 257) and, accordingly, considers *Being and Time* to be the pivotal text, though not for the usual reason. Sheehan wants "to retire the world 'temporality' from Heidegger scholarship ... when speaking of the thrown-open ('ex-static') disclosedness of ex-sistence" (Sheehan 2015, 169).

I find such an account implausible for two reasons. First, Sheehan's retranslation of basic Heideggerian terms seems motivated by his more general re-interpretation of Heidegger's work, rather than the other way around. For example, Sheehan substitutes "the clearing" for "the merely formal indicative 'das Sein Selbst' [Being itself]" in a quotation "to avoid the ambiguity in Heidegger's use of 'das Sein'" (Sheehan 2015, 199n31; my interpolation). To avoid ambiguity by forcing a unitary meaning is questionable, at best. Although Heidegger himself occasionally indulges in the same kind of circular maneuver, it remains in need of independent justification, which I find largely lacking in Sheehan (and often in Heidegger). Moreover, while I share Sheehan's discomfort with the quasi-mystical role that

Being plays in the work of some second- and third-generation Heideggerians, to identify Being with "the clearing" could easily be seen as placing it on the same plane as Dasein. Such "leveling" seems to me profoundly un-Heideggerian.

The second problem is more closely tied to the larger argument here. Sheehan sees Heidegger's work on technology and his engagement with science as severable from the rest of his philosophy. Sheehan claims it follows from Heidegger's own position that "there is *in principle no limit* to what we can know about the knowable and do with the doable. There should be no shrinking back from the human will, no looking askance at the scientific and technological achievements of existential subjects in the modern world" (Sheehan 2015, 209). He describes Heidegger's critique of modern technology as "meta-history" that "has about as much explanatory power as does the Christian story of original sin" (Sheehan 2015, 287–88). It is, frankly, difficult to know what to make of this claim in the face of the way Heidegger weaves his argument against technology with, for example, his discussion of the concept of *Ereignis* in the "Postscript to 'What is Metaphysics'" (Heidegger 1998, 231–38). It is almost as if Sheehan wants to jettison the technology texts primarily because of their susceptibility to a variety of superficial dismissals.

In my view, by contrast, the work on technology flows from Heidegger's earliest preoccupations. The point about the "age of the world picture" is not its products in the material realm, but its insistence on "man" as "the relational center of that which is as such" (Heidegger 1977, 128). This may be a metahistorical claim, but its explanatory force does not come from what it has to say about the ontic phenomena of technology, but from what it says about how Dasein understands itself in relation to Being. That would make it part of the core of Heidegger's thought (and a large part of his legacy for praxis) and integral to the dialectic of arrogance and humility that I find in Heidegger's work.[2] Sheehan's use of "human being," while carefully nuanced, taken in connection with the identification of Being with "the clearing," feels like a repetition of "the loss of the gods" (Heidegger 1977, 116) and a return to the humanism or anthropocentrism that I believe Heidegger moved beyond.

III: Deconstruction After *Destrucktion*

> The cat's universe is not the universe of an anthill. The truism "All thought is anthropomorphic" has no other meaning.
>
> —Albert Camus (*The Myth of Sisyphus*, 1991)

Geschlecht

Derrida's work is discussed more at length here because, while my basic orientation to Heidegger came from my graduate work with Dreyfus, my orientation toward philosophy as whole is based on Derrida's deconstruction of the metaphysical tradition. I previously invoked his first article that engages directly with Heidegger, "*Ousia* and *Grammé*," from 1968. It was another fifteen years before Derrida returned to an explicit critique of Heidegger's thought. I emphasize an "explicit critique" because much of what he wrote before and after the *Geschlecht* articles can be read as tacit critiques, albeit deeply grounded in Heidegger's ideas. It is worthy of note, moreover, that the two *Geschlecht* articles also invoke gender issues—the subtitle of "*Geschlecht* I" is "Sexual Difference, Ontological Difference"—a subject that was also implicit in his work as early as *Of Grammatology* in 1967. However, the role of gender in Derrida's thought did not become explicit until the 1981 interview with Christie V. McDonald that was published as "Choreographies."[3] That these two discourses—on Heidegger and on gender—should be interwoven in this way is not, as Derrida might say, an accident. In any event, I will first look at the two texts on *Geschlecht*; then at another text from the 1980s that engages Heidegger directly, *Of Spirit* (sometimes referred to as "*Geschlecht* III"); and next at a later text that comes from the perspective of body in lieu of mind, *On Touching—Jean-Luc Nancy* (which bridges the 1990s). Finally, I will move to Derrida's critique of Heidegger's attitude toward animals as revealed in the lectures published as *The Beast and the Sovereign, Volume II*.[4]

(*Das*) *Geschlecht* is a German noun that can mean sex/gender, but also "race, family, generation, lineage, species, genre." Derrida begins this reading of Heidegger with the observations that "Heidegger speaks as little as possible" of sex (Derrida 2008, 7), that he insists on the gender neutrality of the term "Dasein" (Derrida 2008, 10), and that he limits the number of sexes to two (Derrida 2008, 12). Given what I have been arguing here, it is not surprising that Derrida sees the supposed neutrality of Dasein not as a strict sexlessness, but rather as a "pre-dual sexuality" that might lie beyond the mind/body distinction (though Derrida does not specifically say this). Derrida does say that this sexlessness (*Geschlechtlosigkeit*) "would not be more negative than *alētheia*." For Heidegger, he explains, this neutrality "is not the void of an abstraction; rather, it leads back to the 'potency of origin' that bears in itself the intrinsic possibility of humanity in its concrete facticity" (Derrida 2008, 14–15). What Derrida finds problematic is exactly what my reading of Heidegger would lead us to expect: "Every body is sexed, and there is no *Dasein* without bodiliness. But ... the dispersing multiplicity is not primarily due to the sexuality of the body; it is bodiliness itself, the flesh, the *Leiblichkeit*, that originally draws Dasein into dispersion and *thus* into sexual difference" (Derrida 2008, 18). In other words, sex/gender is part of the world in which we find ourselves and, as such, is uniquely tied to the body we encounter there as ours. With all due recognition for the history of abuse regarding the concept of gender neutrality (from which Heidegger is not exempt), one is left with at least two options. Either sexual difference is ontological, on a level with the difference between Dasein and beings, or sexual difference, like the body/mind dichotomy and all the replacements and displacements on both sides of this opposition, belong to Dasein in the world and not to Dasein as the empty, open source of meaning. It is this latter option, I believe, that Derrida does not fully appreciate here.

Interpreting Heidegger's text in this second way would also explain how Heidegger can deny the primordiality of sexual *difference* without necessarily denying the possibility Derrida suggests by asking, "What if 'sexuality' already marked the most originary *Selbstheit*?" (Derrida 2008, 17). If being-a-self, and hence a sexual self, held a different place in Heidegger's thought than the traditional view of gender neutrality that Derrida wants to find in his text, one would, among other things, find it easier to understand the gender-fluidity of being-a-self. But Derrida follows another path here, one that questions whether leaving sex/gender to be "deduced" from a prior genderlessness is "to confirm the most traditional philosophemes by repeating them with the force of new rigor?" Derrida's path also leads back to *Being and Time*, "the mode-of-being of the *living*" (Derrida 2008, 22–23; his emphasis), and the problem of the animal that organizes the critique of Heidegger in *The Beast and the Sovereign*.

"Heidegger's Hand (*Geschlecht II*)" begins not with sexual difference, but with "the problem of man, of man's humanity, and of humanism" (Derrida 2008, 30; the context is a reading of Fichte, so "man" is *das Menschlichkeit*). This is the realm of *Geschlecht* as "race." Derrida notes the link between racism and the biologism that Heidegger never failed to condemn, even in the Rectorship Address. The concept of Geschlecht as sex/gender, race, and species leads Derrida to discuss the monster, which fails to belong to a proper species, and then the link in French between monster and *montrer* (to show or point out) and *la montre* (a watch) (Derrida 2008, 32–33).[5] For Derrida, "Heidegger's Hand" refers to the distinction Heidegger wants to make between technē as the work of the hand and modern technology. This is a hierarchical dualism found throughout Heidegger's work (Derrida 2008, 36–38), as is the opposition between the animal and the human, another form of biologism (Derrida 2008, 40). Moreover, just as he assumes two sexes, Heidegger insists on the singular hand (Derrida 2008, 49). In this context, Derrida notes that "I never 'criticize' Heidegger without recalling that this can be done from other places in his own text. His text is not homogeneous, and it is written with two hands, at least" (Derrida 2008, 57).

Spirit and (the) Touch

Geschlecht, thus, encompasses a wide range of problems that Derrida finds in Heidegger—some that arise directly in Heidegger's texts (e.g., humanism); some linked to major themes in his work (biologism as a version of scientism and as reflected in the philosophies of life he rejects); some mentioned "as little as possible" (sex/gender); and some implicit in the other points, most notably race and a biology of "race" that remains more European than American.[6] *Of Spirit* engages directly with the latter point in the same way that the articles on *Geschlecht* address the first three points, and it does so in conjunction with a concept closely tied to my argument, *Geist*, or spirit, another term Heidegger "avoids." In *Being and Time*, Heidegger warns directly that we must avoid that term (Derrida 1981, 1). However, Derrida insists that Heidegger continues to use the term and its cognates.[7] Derrida also asks what it means to "avoid" something, especially in the case of Heidegger and in the context in which Derrida sets this text. That context is one of flame (the symbol of the holy spirit, though Derrida does not say so explicitly) and ashes (and ovens)—hence in relation to Heidegger and race, a tacitly political one as well. This critique also has strong resonances with the interpretation of Heidegger I have offered. The warning in *Being and Time*, Derrida notes, means that Dasein has to be seen as something other than some kind of "*spiritual* interiority," and "one must not say that being-in-a-world ... is a spiritual property" (Derrida 1989, 24; his emphasis). Heidegger also uses the words "spirit" and "spiritual" in quotation marks there. These are generally negative usages, Derrida notes, though some are "scare quotes" that suggest "another appellation, unless it alter the same word, the same appellation, unless it re-call the other under the same."

In the Rectorship Address, however, "spirit" is present in full force in "the self-affirmation of the German university" (Derrida 2008, 29–31), while at the same time Heidegger attempts to separate the term from its Christian implications (Derrida 2008, 33). Derrida offers several explanations for Heidegger's use of the term in this text, including the fact that "one cannot demarcate oneself from biologism, from naturalism, from racism in its genetic form [as understood in Heidegger's time], one cannot be *opposed* to them except by reinscribing spirit in an oppositional determination." This links humanism in the form of human rights not only to spirit, but also to a certain subject/subjectivity, the dangers of which are clear to both Heidegger and Derrida (Derrida 2008, 39–40; his emphasis). The next chapter of Derrida's book moves from humanism in this form to Heidegger's claim in the Freiburg lectures of 1929–30 that "the animal is poor in world." Derrida takes this claim to mean, "It is not that the animal has a lesser relationship, a more limited access to entities, it has an *other* relationship" (Derrida 2008, 49; his emphasis), In Edelman's terms, it lacks second-order consciousness. Thus, its "poverty" is different in kind from the "*self*-destitution" of Dasein in the modern age (Derrida 2008, 63; his emphasis).

Derrida does not linger there in this text. He raises the question of the relationship between spirit and psyché (Derrida 2008, 74), pointing out that in talking about spirit, psyché, and *pneuma* in St. Paul, Heidegger has "*incorporated the translation of at least one language and of a historicality which is here never* named, never thought." The missing words in Heidegger are the Hebrew *ruah* (St Paul's *pneuma*) and *néphéch* (psyché) (Derrida 2008, 101–2; his emphasis). The understanding of *Geschlecht* as "race" has finally become explicit—"Nazism was not born in the desert" (Derrida 2008, 109). Spirit may, thus, be a necessary concept in some contexts, given the need to oppose some form of humanism or human rights to racial, ethnic, religious, and other forms of oppression. However, the undoing of the mind/body dyad that I am suggesting might in the end provide another way to undo the damage to ourselves and our world that has been done by the concept of spirit and its cognates during the past twenty centuries.

In the same way that the concept of spirit touches on, but does not fully engage, the relationship between mind and body under discussion, *On Touching—Jean-Luc Nancy* flirts with the dichotomy of inner and outer, especially with regard to the lips and the kiss. This is a quintessentially Gallic gesture that the Algerian-born Derrida apparently never became entirely comfortable with (Derrida 2005, 302). This text also discusses the (female) figure of the goddess *Psyché* in Nancy's work (as well as Aristotle's), and it engages precisely with the inner/outer in the work of Descartes, for whom sensations (including those of touch) are ideas and, hence, "spiritual and not at all corporeal." (Derrida notes that "this would be the same for the analogous moment in Husserl's phenomenology" [Derrida 2005, 31]). He also uses a text by Immanuel Levinas to close the circle of *Geschlecht*, by tying sex/gender directly to the animal: "There is an implacable configuration there [in Levinas]: femininity, infancy, animality, irresponsibility" (Derrida 2005, 87; my interpolation). He asks if we are "straining the point by restricting the traits of this truly hierarchizing discourse [Levinas's] to this 'masculine civilization,' which is precisely in question here, which is *naturally* in question in this analysis of … the 'epiphany of the feminine'?" (Derrida 2005, 89; his emphasis, my interpolation). Moreover, in a footnote, he notes an echo of the argument of *Geschlecht* in Didier Franck's *Chair et corps:* "It is because reckoning with the flesh—fleshly, or sexual, difference—would have jeopardized the privilege of temporality that Heidegger is said to have kept to a sexually neutral *Dasein.*" He cites, as I have, Heidegger's conclusion in *On Time and Being:* "The attempt, in *Being and Time,* section 70, to derive human spatiality [of *Dasein*—trans.] from temporality is untenable" (Derrida 2005, 359).

The thread I would like to follow in *On Touching* is not unrelated to *Of Spirit.* This thread includes Derrida's engagement with Nancy's project of deconstructing Christianity and, indirectly, with the possibility of Heidegger's attempt to return to a Greek thought before Christianity, especially in regard to the mind/body dichotomy. Derrida states, "Only Christianity can do this work, that is, undo it while doing it. Heidegger, too—Heidegger already—has only succeeded in failing at this" (Derrida 2005, 54). This necessary failure is due to the fact that "a certain Christianity will always take charge of the most exacting, the most *exact,* and the most eschatological hyperbole of deconstruction, the overbid of 'Hoc est enim corpus meum' ['Here is my body']" (Derrida 2005, 60; my interpolation). A question he poses to Nancy could also be posed to Heidegger, and links this text to Derrida's other writings on the relationship between "the West" and that which is outside it but always touching it:[8]

> Shall one join him [Nancy] when he says that this history of the world and the body is merely Christian, or even Abrahamic, and limited to the West ('principle of (un)reason of the West')? And to the body 'for us,' implying 'we,' the Jewish, Christian, or Muslim heirs of 'Hoc enim corpus meum,' as the beginning of the text suggest it? Or is it a universal 'history'? Or further, in greater likelihood, the history of the production of every 'universalism' and 'globalization'—through the obligatory passage of a surreptitious, autoimmune, and globalatinizing Christianization? (Derrida 2005, 63–64; my interpolations)[9]

For Derrida, the history Nancy invokes is universal/global, because it has been imposed on other peoples by European Christianity through military conquest built on an ideology of saving the souls/spirits/minds of those enslaved/killed. This is an auto-deconstruction of the hierarchical dichotomies on which the tradition is built and which both Heidegger and Derrida argue against.

In both Nancy's text and Derrida's, touch destabilizes mind/body dualism and all its cognate hierarchical dichotomies. Derrida quotes Nancy as saying, "it is not we who decide whether this will be the task of philosophy" (an echo of Heidegger), but rather "if philosophy has *touched the limit* [my emphasis—J.D.] of the ontology of subjectivity, this is because it has been led to this limit."[10] Derrida adds, "There is thus, apparently, a *figure of* touch there, for philosophy, literally, has never touched anything. Above all, nobody, no body, no body proper has ever touched—with a hand or through skin contact—something as abstract as a limit. Inversely, however, and that is the destiny of this figurality, all one ever does touch is a limit" (Derrida 2005, 103; his emphasis, his interpolation). If the mouth or the kiss previously mentioned (and not unrelated to the spirit of Christian betrayal) evokes an outside/inside, touch is also an inside/outside, the point where the difference between self/body and its other is most clear. However, they must be sufficiently similar to touch. For Descartes, this sameness is mental/spiritual (because sensations are ideas), but it also belongs to extension. Descartes is, after all, the mathematician of the limit, of the touch that approaches without touching in a space that exists outside of the mind, which it touches only at one point deep within the brain. Even the great dualist could not keep the outside out of the inside and vice versa. Derrida notes earlier that "the lexicon of touch … carries a semantic tenor whose specter seems to obey a subtle and ironic play, both discreet and virtuoso. As if a master of language airily made believe he wasn't touching any of it. And by the way, is he doing it on purpose? Or is he letting a treacherous symptom show an obsession too strong to be dominated or formalized? A dread that is within language before it haunts the individual subject?" Derrida is speaking of Nancy here, but earlier on the same page, he notes that "one can never forget this Christian (Lutheran, Pascalian, Hegelian, Kierkegaardian, Marxian, and so forth) memory when one reads Heidegger, when one also questions his denials" (Derrida 2005, 60).

The Beast

In the context of the ways in which Heidegger, Nancy, and Descartes remain captive to the languages in which they find themselves, Derrida cites Paul de Man's emendation of "language speaks" (*Die Sprache spricht*) as "*Die Sprache verspicht*" (language promises) and, later, as "*Die Sprache verspicht sich*" (language promises itself): "language or speech promises, promises *itself* but also goes back on its word … just as immediately and just as essentially" (Derrida 1989, 93–94; his emphasis). *The Beast and the Sovereign* makes much the same point with regard to Heidegger's reading of "Antigone" in *Introduction to Metaphysics* (1935):

> But what one forgets … is that man is seized, gripped, *durchwalten* [roughly, overpowered] by the *Gewalt* [literally, power] of this *Walten* [roughly, power], and it is because one forgets this and attributes to this man, as to a subject, the initiative or the invention of language, of comprehension, etc.—this is why man had paradoxically become a stranger ([*unheimisch*], uncanny this time) to his own essence. Because he believes he is the author, the master and possessor, and the inventor of these powers, he ignores the fact that he is first of all griped, seized, that he must take them on, and he then becomes basically a foreigner—this is the whole story—to his own *Unheimlichkeit*. (Derrida 2011, 288; translators' interpolation in parentheses, mine in brackets)[11,12]

Derrida's main interest appears to be with what he sees as a political subtext centered on the word *Walten*, which could be translated as "rule" (in the sense of government) or "sovereignty." Thus, Derrida highlights Heidegger's references to *Walten* in *Introduction to Metaphysics* as physis, *logos*, and *eidos*: "From then on, says Heidegger, the interpretation of Being as idea dominates (*beherrscht* [from *beherrschen*, to rule or govern]) the whole of Western thought, up to Hegel and beyond. And the idealism that then dominates Western metaphysics through and through is a determination of violence."

The tie between this idea and Derrida's concern with the status of the "beast" in Heidegger can be seen when he notes that the only thing that can cause this violence to *scheitert* (German for founder or become a wreck—these lectures focus on *Robinson Crusoe*) is death. The question, then, is one of "who can die?" (Derrida 2011, 290). Death, of course, serves in *Being and Time* as one of the ways in which Dasein is distinguished from other living things: "The ending of that which lives we have called 'perishing.' Dasein too 'has' its death of the kind appropriate to anything that lives" but still, "*qua* Dasein, it does not simply perish." This is because, authentically or inauthentically, Dasein attaches meaning to its own death. Animals with "first order" consciousness are aware of the world without being aware of themselves. They may, in some cases, be aware of death, and they have an instinctual fear of what can kill them, but that does not amount, Heidegger suggests, to an awareness of themselves as beings that will die. That kind of "second order" consciousness is reserved for Dasein. Thus, the topic of *The Beast and the Sovereign* is what sets Dasein apart from other sorts of beings.

In *Being and Time* Heidegger notes the truth, on some level, of the scientific understanding of both life and death. But he insists that underneath this "biological-ontical exploration of death is a problematic that is ontological," because "the ontology of Dasein" is "superordinate to an ontology of life" (Heidegger 1962, 291). This idea reflects the larger distinction that Heidegger makes between Dasein and animals, based on his belief that the being of beings as such depends on the existence of Dasein as an entity that can understand them as the beings they are in a meaningful world. One of the horizons of that world is constituted by the death that only Dasein knows awaits it. If one accepts Derrida's argument that this key distinction in Heidegger fails, or is irremediably contaminated by Heidegger's admittedly heinous politics (at least in the early 1930s), then my argument here must also fail in several ways.

Derrida offers challenges to Heidegger's thought on a wide range of other topics that fall outside the scope of this project. While I find many, if not most, of his arguments valuable and often persuasive, Derrida's preoccupation with the status of animals has never felt compelling to me.[13] I have always sensed that somehow he was missing Heidegger's point, but only now that I have come to a fuller understanding of what that point was can I articulate my reservations.

I believe that Derrida's concerns arise from three sources—two more specific than a general distrust of Heidegger's politics and one more abstract. One source is Derrida's own interactions with the animals he encounters in his life, a topic I will return to later. A more specific source of Derrida's critique has previously been mentioned—the potential loss of a concept of human or humanity that could ground moral and political values such a concept of human rights. Clearly, such a loss brings a wealth of dangers in its wake, many of which might be grouped under the heading of "what counts as a human"—or "who can die" (or be killed). Given Heidegger's political history, the move to decouple Dasein from the biologically human and to "downgrade" the nonhuman animal might seem ominous. Added to the third source—the fact that the dichotomy human/animal is deeply steeped in the onto-theological metaphysics that Heidegger wants to avoid at all costs—there is much room for discomfort here, and I would never want to minimize it.

What I am trying to do, though, is what Derrida does elsewhere (e.g., in *Of Spirit*). I am thinking through Heidegger in a way that recognizes the dangers while at the same time noting the assumption behind the discomfort. Here, that assumption is the unstated belief that if animals are "less" than Dasein, they do not deserve respect as the beings they indeed are. Yet, while on a personal level it might make sense for Heidegger to have great reverence for the Rhine River but consider animals of no worth, it is hard to believe he would engage in such a simple and obvious contradiction.[14] If we are to adopt an attitude toward physis closer to the Greeks', we must develop more reverence for the beings it gives us, including both rivers *and* animals. It is a result of the very humanism Derrida and Heidegger question that we assume anything "less than" human deserves no respect.

As I have done here, Derrida largely sets aside *Being and Time* in his discussion because "to my knowledge, then, the concept and vocabulary of *Walten* is not at work—at least not centrally—in *Sein und Zeit*" (Derrida 2011, 43). He also acknowledges that when Heidegger says in "Origin of the Work of Art" (1935), "The stone is worldless. Plant and animal likewise have no world; but they belong to the covert throng of a surrounding into which they are linked" (Heidegger 1993, 170), or in *Introduction to Metaphysics*, "The animal has no world (*Welt*) nor any environment (*Umwelt*)" (Heidegger 2000, 47), "Heidegger's point is less to say something essential about the stone, the animal, or man than to say something essential about differences *as to the world*" (Derrida, 2011, 57; his emphasis). In the discussion that follows, Derrida links the concept of world in Heidegger with the metaphor of a path (*Weg*).[15] Later, Derrida finds much more in the image of a path than a metaphor, and does so by interpreting Heidegger in a way that parallels my argument: "this *Weg* and this *bewegen* [i.e., to set on a path] are not simply metaphors, in that they engage Dasein before any distinction between soul and body" because they are part of Dasein's unthematized, everyday interactions with what is "ready to hand" (Derrida 2011, 91; my interpolation).

Derrida also agrees with the account of the relative status of science and ontology in Heidegger's work as previously outlined, but he adds, with uncharacteristic regard for the scientific enterprise, that Heidegger's position "comes down to discrediting scientific knowledge with respect to certain questions the reply to which is supposedly presupposed by science, precisely—this disqualification of science will be for us a locus of problematization, of course" (Derrida 2011, 109). Given Derrida's work as a whole, one cannot take this comment as a championing of science, but rather as a rejection of Heidegger's preference for ontology over science, a hierarchy that can too easily evoke the reign of onto-theology at its worse.[16]

Derrida seems to understand Heidegger's motives more or less as I interpret them. In one session of these lectures, but not in his notes for it, he states the following:

> And this is what Heidegger would like to, let's say, deconstruct: the determination of man primarily as a living being and not as a mortal [i.e., a being who will die]. On the basis of life and living, and there it's *Leben* [life] *und Erleben* [usually, experience or adventure—cf. re *Robinson Crusoe*], and for my part I read in this ... an implicit critique or an implicit reservation specifically about Husserl, and phenomenology that determines its phenomenological absolute as *Erlebnis*, as life, transcendental life; *Leben und Erleben*; if he adds *und Erleben*, it's because he has in mind, he's taking critical aim at, the determination of Being a life, the human absolute as living, and thereby phenomenology as a philosophy of life, of transcendental life. Which I also tried to question long ago (Derrida, 2011, 124; the reference is to his book on Husserl, *Speech and Phenomena*).

Derrida links these comments to the point made earlier about the German university. He acknowledges Heidegger's concern to avoid both anthropomorphism and anthropocentrism, but then notes Heidegger's tendency to lump all animals together "*with respect to human Dasein.*" He grants that Heidegger's claim that animals are "poor in world" might be about "the limits of *this* world that Dasein has formed or configured for itself," but then asks, "But are not the limits of this world thus configured the very thing one must try to cross in order to *think*?" (Derrida 2011, 196–98; his emphasis). The implication here, and elsewhere, appears to be that if Heidegger rejected the last vestiges of onto-theology and crossed the limits of the Western world's understanding of what an animal is, he might have begun to "think"—that is, to philosophize beyond philosophy.

I would argue, however, that Heidegger is precisely thinking in that sense about animals. I have previously noted that one of Derrida's motives for this discussion lies in his everyday encounters with animals, encounters suggesting that the animals are not somehow literally "subhuman"—that is, like us but "deprived" of an order of consciousness, of the ability to take things "as such" (Derrida 2011, 200–201). Rather, the encounters suggest that animals may have *other ways* of ordering their experience and, hence, are merely non-human. No one who has ever met the disdainful stare of a cat or the patient gaze of a dog in pain can deny that such encounters can be uncanny in the full Heideggerian sense of the word. I would argue that their uncanniness arises not from the possibility of another point of view on the world we share, but from the possibility of existing in that world without having a point of view at all. To borrow a phrase from Thomas Nagel, I cannot know what it is like to be a bat, or a cat, or a dog not only because of the differences in how their perceptual fields are organized, but also because I cannot know what it is like not to be aware that

I *am* a bat or a cat or a dog. The bat, cat, or dog has a perceptual field, but cannot know it as *its own* or as belonging to a meaningful perceptual world. Second-order consciousness makes all the difference in our relation to beings and in our relation to Being.

Two recent books address the same point in light of contemporary research in animal psychology and biology. Frans de Waal answers the question of his title, *Are We Smart Enough to Know How Smart Animals Are?*, in the affirmative and goes on to say, as I have here, that the usual dualism of "body and mind, human and animal, or reason and emotion" are not helpful in the study of what he calls "animal cognition" (Waal 2016, 5). As strong a Darwinian as Edelman, de Waal insists, "Each organism has its own ecology and lifestyle, its own *Umwelt*, which dictates what it needs to know in order to make a living" (Waal 2016, 267). Rather than intelligence being like a ladder with humans at the top, the inside front cover of his book states, "it is more like a bush, with cognition taking different forms that are quite incomparable to ours." While de Waal likens animal and human cognition, he clearly differentiates human and animal consciousness on the points central to Heidegger's position. After denying that even great apes can understand death in the abstract, much less anticipate their own, de Waal states, "You won't often hear me say something like this, but I consider us the only linguistic species." Moreover, he locates at least part of the reason for this uniqueness in the fact that animal communication "is almost entirely restricted to the here and now" (Waal 2016, 106).

Biologist Nathan Lents takes a similarly evolutionary standpoint in *Not So Different: Finding Human Nature in Animals*. His focus is on the "basic behavioral scaffolding" that humans share "with most other social animals," though he acknowledges from the outset "our abilities in advanced reasoning, which we all agree exceed those of other animals" (Lents 2016, 2). Lents also describes animal attitudes toward death in terms of grieving, not awareness of the organism's own death, and he demarcates human from animal consciousness in terms of language: "I think both humans and chimpanzees feel love; the only difference is that humans write sonnets about it. I think both humans and dolphins practice fair play, but only humans enact laws to govern it" (Lents 2016, 15).

As we saw in the earlier discussion of artificial intelligence, this entire line of thought in fact begs the question as to the relevance of science to the study of human consciousness. However, it also seems that the latest scientific thinking on animal consciousness tends to come down on Heidegger's side in this dispute. Despite the tantalizing titles of these books, the issue between his view and Derrida's view is not how "smart" animals are or how much their brains or their behaviors are like ours. Rather, the main issue is whether animals have the same kind of consciousness as Dasein—that is, the way they relate to Being. No possible science can give us an answer to that question.[17]

To protect ourselves from the temptation to treat animals badly simply because they are animals—which appears to be Derrida's aim—we need to keep two points in mind. (Note that these points apply *mutatis mutandis* to other humans that we may be tempted to regard in a lesser light.) First, as previously noted, we owe respect, protection, and even reverence to *all* beings, not just Dasein: to animals, to the natural world as a whole, and to physis. I think this is quite clear in Heidegger.[18] This means that we must question the destruction of rainforests to create palm oil plantations for the sake of the rainforest *itself*, not only because of the impact of habitat loss on local orangutan populations. To put this point another way, we must be as morally concerned with our unsustainable double shot soy latte as with our unsustainable hamburgers. Secondly, we *cannot* know what it is like to be a bat. Animal experience is irretrievably cut off from our knowing. This is a necessary, even ontological ignorance that shows not our superiority to animals, but our finitude.[19] And that, I would argue, makes all the difference between Heidegger and the tradition of onto-theology.

Notes

1. I would like to thank my Hamline colleague Mark Berkson for calling my attention to Sheehan's book.

2. For a fuller explanation of this claim, see Holland, *Ontological Humility*.

3. Reprinted in Holland, *Feminist Interpretations of Jacques Derrida*.

4. The original piece that forms the basis of *On Touching* was written in 1992, but the book was published in 2000.

5. In the move from gender to species to monster, one might remember that Aristotle, so revered by Heidegger, finds it reasonable to ask in the *Metaphysics*, "why woman does not differ from man in species" (Iota 9, 1058a30).

6. Which is not to say, of course, that the United States does not have its own problems with race. For more on the difference, cf. Ladelle McWhorter's *Racism and Sexual Oppression in Anglo-America*.

7. Derrida does not give page references to Heidegger in this text.

8. For example, in sections of *The Beast and the Sovereign, Volume II* that we are unable to discuss here.

9. As usual in philosophy, both Nancy and Derrida ignore both the fact that the three nations with the largest Muslim populations are neither in, nor touch on, "the West." This suggests that even for them, "the Abrahamic traditions" remains, as Derrida indicates in what he said about the status of Hebrew (above), a code word for Christianity.

10. Derrida is quoting Nancy, *The Experience of Freedom* (p. 7), translation slightly modified in Derrida's text.

11. For good reasons, the translators of Derrida's text leave *Walten* and its cognates in German; my interpolations are the merest approximation of how Derrida interprets them for those unfamiliar with these lectures.

12. "*Unheimisch*" is corrected from *uneinheimisch* in a footnote to Derrida's text.

13. For a general comparison of Heidegger's work and Derrida's work, see my *The Madwoman's Reason* (1998).

14. One could argue that it is what the Rhine represents to the German people, not the river itself, that Heidegger reveres, but his similar regard for the Danube in *Hölderlin's Hymn "The Ister"* suggests that it is the river, its history, and the landscape it carves, as much as what it represents, that he respects.

15. This path is also linked to Heidegger's account of *pragma* in *Parmenides*, discussed in chapter 7.

16. The current popularity of "creation science" and climate change denial in its overtly and covertly religious forms prove that this "at its worst" is not a thing of the past.

17. A recent article by Antonino Firenze, "A Dog Does Not Exist But Merely Lives: The Question of Animality in Heidegger's Philosophy," makes the same mistake. Firenze concludes, "Heidegger failed to understand the link between humanity and animality, precisely because he failed to consider this link in terms of a deeper bond between natural life and human existence—a bond that represents one of the most pressing milestones in contemporary philosophical thinking." But Firenze never questions the relationship between that "milestone" (presumably evolutionary theory) and the scientific-technological modernity that Heidegger sought throughout his career to decenter from how we understand our existence as Dasein.

18. On this, see Holland, *Ontological Humility*.

19. See Holland, *Ontological Humility* on this point as well.

Conclusion: "Ψυχή Being Not a Soul but the Unmediated Discovery of Being"

We shall no longer hold that perception is incipient science, but conversely that classical science is a form of perceptions which loses sight of its origins and believes itself complete.

—Maurice Merleau-Ponty (*Phenomenology of Perception*, 1962).

In CHAPTER 1, I set three goals for this project. The first goal was to provide a coherent account of how Heidegger understood and sought to solve the problem of consciousness, as laid out in chapter 2. My second goal was to offer an explanation of why this major thread in Heidegger's thought has been systematically missed or misunderstood. Finally, by basing my account on the full range of his work, my third goal was to suggest a more unified interpretation of his writings, if not one that would allow us to, in Sheehan's terms, "make sense" of them. None of these objectives fit well with the currently dominant understanding of Heidegger's work, which has its roots, at least in North America, in the teachings of a relatively small number of scholars who found refuge here roughly eighty years ago (well before the end of Heidegger's career). As an outsider to this tradition, I do not pretend to understand his work better than those scholars who knew and studied with him. Instead, I hope to bring new possibilities into the conversation with their students, who now carry the torch. This is a purpose I believe I share with Dreyfus, Capobianco, Sheehan, Derrida, and many of my peer feminist Heideggerians.[1] As this generation of scholars reaches the end of our careers, it is time for a new phalanx (a properly Greek word Heidegger might appreciate) to move forward. This book is meant to suggest one way in which the next generation might do that.

Part of that new direction is the conviction I share with Sheehan that, although without an ethics in the usual sense, Heidegger's work is deeply moral at its core. Sheehan calls this the "protreptic" moment in Heidegger (Sheehan 2015, 155). As previously explained, this is why I believe Sheehan misses the point of Heidegger's work on technology—he sees it as an ontic, historical account.

In my view, Heidegger's concern in not the "truth" about technology, but what might become of Dasein if technology is allowed to be the only way in which we understand the world and if "*Being* means always and everywhere: the Being of *beings*" (Heidegger 2002b, 61; his emphasis).

The reading of the full range of Heidegger's work, as offered here, is meant to establish that how we understand beings, how we understand Dasein, and how we understand the relationship between the two—that is, the status of science and the problem of consciousness—were already subjects central to his lectures before *Being and Time* and the *Kehre*. These concepts are deeply linked to his critique of the traditional understanding of intentionality, as well as to his critique of technology; they are also deeply linked to each other. My claim is that one cannot talk about the world of science in Heidegger without also talking about Dasein. Moreover, his persistent attempt to break through the mind/body, subject/object dichotomy implies a radical reconceptualization of the relationship between Dasein and material reality that might yet save us from technology.

All of this is hidden in plain sight in Heidegger's text. As we have seen, Dasein primarily lives in a world that is meaningful because it is social. Within that world, other kinds of beings and their specific properties become salient such that Dasein questions them in their essence. In time, Dasein also comes to question itself. "This foundation happened in the West for the first time in Greece" (Heidegger 1993, 201).[2] There, this questioning took the form of investigating objects and their attributes, initially for pragmatic purposes but eventually for the sake of investigation itself. Christianity gave the emphasis on the difference between knower and known, body and soul, a new urgency. With Protestantism, certainty (of grace) became a vital question. From this arose the Cartesian mind/body dualism that underlies modern science (e.g., Heidegger 2003, 13–14). This science is, however, barred in fact and in principle from taking Dasein—human questioning itself—as its object, because the world that science studies is a manifestation of, and exists as such only for, consciousness. Heidegger's formulation of the change that needs to be made is already clear in the note cited from *The Essence of Truth*: "(commonly: 'object'–'subject'; actually: manifestness, understanding of being)" (Heidegger 2002a, 81). This conceptual shift is one of Heidegger's abiding preoccupations.

Of course, the complications of such a shift are many. As embodied, Dasein is *part of* the natural world (a topic Derrida returns to often, if often indirectly). In addition, the "facts" about nature that form the basis for science are "facts" only in the context of the concepts that Dasein uses to investigate nature. The passage of time has caused other shifts, both conceptual and material. From one perspective, more optimism about our future might be warranted now that the danger of technology no longer necessarily takes the immediate form of a nuclear apocalypse. Whatever else might be said about global warming, it is a gradually increasing danger, from which human intervention might yet rescue what Heidegger would consider the most essential elements of life as we know it. Nuclear annihilation requires only one Dr. Strangelove, while the disasters brought by global warming require millions of daily acts of greed, ignorance, and stupidity. This suggests a perspective in which we might be less optimistic about our future—even less optimistic than Heidegger was. He suggested that a god might save us, but it seems more likely that our salvation can come only from a myriad of acts and choices made by people across the globe. Such "little things" (Heidegger 1977, 33) can be generated by conversions from the arrogance of technology to the humility that reflects our true relationship to Being, to the beings around us, and to each other.

What remains supremely clear across almost fifty-five years of Heidegger's thought is the growth of the danger that he warned us of in 1919—"We stand at an abyss: either into nothingness, that is, absolute reification, pure thingness, or we somehow leap into *another world*" (Heidegger 2008, 51; his emphasis). The excesses of technology affect the natural world (from the dam on the Rhine River to irreversible climate change), the human world (from the Nazi prison camp to the "blood diamond" mines of contemporary Africa), and, more importantly, those realms where both of these worlds are reduced to nothing more than the source of interchangeable parts for the standing reserve (e.g., the treatment of animals, our physical environment, agricultural workers, and consumers in what Heidegger called in 1953 "the mechanized food industry" [Heidegger 1993, 320]). In our obsession with beings, we have lost sight of Being, and we increasingly risk losing sight of Dasein and the possibilities it represents. Since science has appropriated rationality as its own, there is no true argument, no simple account in Heidegger that will make it easier to see the deadly danger of technology—or that will help us overcome this danger to make the leap he envisioned almost a century ago. As Heidegger wrote in 1957, "In this realm one cannot prove any-thing, but one can point out a great deal" (Heidegger 2002b, 22).

Notes

"ψυχή *n'étant pas une âme mais la découverte immediate de l'étant*" (Beaufret 1974, 82, my translation).

1. For examples of feminist work on Heidegger, see Holland and Huntington, *Feminist Interpretations of Martin Heidegger.*

2. Heidegger's Eurocentrism, though invoked at times by Derrida, lies outside the scope of the present argument.

References

Aristotle. 1960. *Metaphysics*. Translated by Richard Hope. Ann Arbor: University of Michigan Press.

———. 1980. *Nicomachean Ethics*. Translated by David Ross. New York: Oxford University Press.

Ayer, Alfred Jules. 1952. *Language, Truth and Logic*. New York: Dover.

Beaufret, Jean. 1974. *Dialogues avec Heidegger*. Paris: Les Editions de Minuit.

Bennington, Geoffrey. 2016. *Scatter 1: The Politics of Politics in Foucault, Heidegger, and Derrida*. New York: Fordham University Press.

Camus, Albert. 1991. *The Myth of Sisyphus and Other Essays*. Translated by Justin O'Brien. New York: Vintage.

Capobianco, Richard. 2014. *Heidegger's Way of Being*. Toronto: University of Toronto Press.

Derrida, Jacques. 1973. *Speech and Phenomena*. Translated by David B. Allison. Evanston, IL: Northwestern University Press

———. 1976. *Of Grammatology*. Translated by Gayatri Chakravorty Spivak. Baltimore: Johns Hopkins University Press.

———. 1982. *Margins: Of Philosophy*. Translated by Alan Bass. Chicago: University of Chicago Press.

———. 1985. "Racism's Last Word," Translated by Peggy Kamuf. *Critical Inquiry* 12, no. 1 (Autumn): 290–99.

———. *Of Spirit*. 1989. Translated by Geoffrey Bennington and Rachel Bowlby. Chicago: University of Chicago Press.

———. 2005. *On Touching—Jean-Luc Nancy*. Translated by Christine Irizarry. Stanford, CA: Stanford University Press.

———. 2008. *Psyche: Inventions of the Other, Volume II*. Edited by Peggy Kamuf and Elizabeth Rottenberg. Stanford, CA: Stanford University Press.

———. 2011. *The Beast and the Sovereign Volume II*. Translated by Geoffrey Bennington. Chicago: University of Chicago Press.

Descartes, René. 1976. *The Philosophical Works of Descartes, Volume I*. Translated by Elizabeth Haldane and G. R. T. Ross. Cambridge, UK: Cambridge University Press.

Dreyfus, Hubert L. 1975. "The Priority of 'The' World to 'My' World: Heidegger's Answer to Husserl (and Sartre)." *Man and World* 8, no. 2: 121–30.

———. 1979. *What Computers Can't Do*. New York: Harper.

———. 1991. *Being-in-the-World: A Commentary on Heidegger's "Being and Time," Division I*. Cambridge, MA: MIT Press.

———. 2006. "Overcoming the Myth of the Mental." *Topoi* 25, no. 2 (September): 43–49.

———. 2007. "Why Heideggerian AI Failed and How Fixing it Would Require Making it More Heideggerian." *Philosophical Psychology* 20, no. 2 (April): 247–68.

Dreyfus, Hubert, and Charles Spinosa. 1999. "Coping with Things-in-Themselves: A Practice-Based Phenomenological Account for Realism." *Inquiry: An Interdisciplinary Journal of Philosophy and the Social Sciences* 42, no. 1: 49–78.

Edelman, Gerald. 1987. *Neural Darwinism: The Theory of Neuronal Group Selection*. New York: Basic Books.

———. 1989. *The Remembered Present: A Biological Theory of Consciousness*. New York: Basic Books.

———. 2006. *Second Nature: Brain Science and Human Knowledge*. New Haven: Yale University Press.

Firenze, Antonino. 2017. "'A Dog Does Not Exist But Merely Lives': The Question of Animality in Heidegger's Philosophy." *Philosophy Today* 61, no. 1 (Winter): 135–54. doi: 10.5840/philtoday201739142.

Foucault, Michel. 1970. *The Order of Things*. Translation unattributed. New York: Vintage.

Grosz, Elizabeth. 2011. "Matter, Life, and Other Variations." *Philosophy Today* 55 (SPEP Supplement): 17–27.

Haar, Michel. 1993. *Heidegger and the Essence of Man*. Translated by William McNeill. Albany: State University of New York Press.

Heidegger, Martin. 1962. *Being and Time*. Translated by John Macquarrie and Edward Robinson. New York: Harper.

———. 1971. *Poetry, Language, Thought*. Translated by Albert Hofstadter. New York: Harper.

———. 1972. *On Time and Being*. Translated by Joan Stambaugh. New York: Harper.

———. 1977. *The Question Concerning Technology and Other Essays*. Translated by William Lovitt. New York: Harper.

———. 1982. *The Basic Problems of Phenomenology*. Translated by Albert Hofstadter. Bloomington: Indiana University Press.

———. 1992. *Parmenides*. Translated by André Schuwer and Richard Rojcewicz. Bloomington: Indiana University Press.

———. 1993. *Basic Writings from "Being and Time" (1927) to "the Task of Thinking" (1964)*. Edited by David Farrell Krell. New York: Harper Collins.

———. 1995. *Aristotle's Metaphysics Θ 1–3*, Translated by Walter Brogan and Peter Warnek. Bloomington: Indiana University Press.

———. 1997. *Plato's Sophist*. Translated by Richard Rojcewicz and André Schwer. Bloomington: Indiana University Press.

———.1998. *Pathmarks*. Edited by William McNeill. Cambridge, UK: Cambridge University Press.

———. 1999. "On the Being and Conception of φύσις in Aristotle's Physics B,1," Translated by Thomas Sheehan. *Man and World* 9, no. 3 (August): 219–79.

———. 2000. *Introduction to Metaphysics*. Translated by Gregory Fried and Richard Polt. New Haven, CT: Yale University Press.

———. 2001. *Phenomenological Interpretations of Aristotle*. Translated by Richard Rojcewicz. Bloomington: Indiana University Press.

———. 2002a. *The Essence of Truth: On Plato's Cave Allegory and Theaetetus*. Translated by Ted Sadler. New York: Continuum.

———. 2002b. *Identity and Difference*. Translated by Joan Stambaugh. Chicago: University of Chicago Press.

———. 2002c. *Supplements: From the Earliest Essays to Being and Time and Beyond*. Edited by John van Buren. Albany: State University of New York Press.

———. 2003. *Four Seminars*. Translated by Andrew Mitchell and François Raffoul. Bloomington: Indiana University Press.

———. 2008. *Towards the Definition of Philosophy.* Translated by Ted Sadler. London: Continuum.

———. 2010. *Logic: The Question of Truth.* Translated by Thomas Sheehan. Bloomington: Indiana University Press.

———. 2012. *Contributions to Philosophy: Of the Event.* Translated by Richard Rojcewicz and Daniela Vallega-Neu. Bloomington: Indiana University Press.

Holland, Nancy J., ed. 1997. *Feminist Interpretations of Jacques Derrida.* University Park: Penn State Press.

———. 1998. *The Madwoman's Reason: The Concept of the Appropriate in Ethical Thought.* University Park: Penn State Press.

———. 2013. *Ontological Humility: Lord Voldemort and the Philosophers.* Albany: State University of New York Press.

———. 2017. "Nature (or Not) in Heidegger." In *Ontologies of Nature: Continental Perspectives and Environmental Reorientations,* edited by Gerard Kuperus and Marjolein Oele, 135–57. Cham, Switzerland: Springer.

Holland, Nancy, and Patricia Huntington, eds. 2001. *Feminist Interpretations of Martin Heidegger.* University Park: Penn State Press.

Kant, Immanuel. 1929. *Critique of Pure Reason.* Translated by Norman Kemp Smith, New York: St. Martin's Press.

———. 2001. *Prolegomena to Any Future Metaphysics.* Translated by James W. Ellington. Indianapolis: Hackett.

Kisiel, Theodore. 1995. *The Genesis of Heidegger's Being and Time.* Berkeley: University of California Press.

Kisiel, Theodore, and John van Buren, eds. 1994. *Reading Heidegger from the Start: Essays in His Earliest Thought.* Albany: State University of New York Press.

Kuhn, Thomas. 1970. *The Structure of Scientific Revolutions.* Chicago: University of Chicago Press.

Lents, Nathan. 2016. *Not So Different: Finding Human Nature in Animals.* New York: Columbia University Press.

Lévi-Strauss, Claude. 1966. *The Savage Mind (La Pensée Sauvage).* Translator unattributed. Chicago: University of Chicago Press.

McWhorter, Ladelle. 2009. *Racism and Sexual Oppression in Anglo-America.* Bloomington: Indiana University Press.

Merleau-Ponty, Maurice. 1962. *Phenomenology of Perception.* Translated by Colin Smith. New York: Routledge.

———. 1964. *Signs.* Translated by Richard C. McCleary. Evanston, IL: Northwestern University Press.

———. 1968. *The Visible and the Invisible.* Translated by Alphonso Lingis. Evanston, IL: Northwestern University Press.

Nagel, Thomas. 1979. *Mortal Questions.* New York: Cambridge University Press.

Nancy, Jean-Luc. 1993. *The Experience of Freedom.* Translated by Bridget McDonald. Stanford, CA: Stanford University Press.

Nietzsche, Friedrich. 1966. *Beyond Good and Evil.* Translated by Walter Kaufman. New York: Vintage.

Noë, Alva. 2007. "Magic Realism and the Limits of Intelligibility: What Makes Us Conscious." *Philosophical Perspectives* 21, no. 1 (December): 457–74.

————. 2009. "Conscious Reference." *The Philosophical Quarterly* 59, no. 236 (July): 470–82.

Olafson, Frederick. 1987. *Heidegger and the Philosophy of Mind*. New Haven, CT: Yale University Press.

Peirce, Charles Sanders. 1955. *Philosophical Writings of Peirce*. Edited by Justus Buchler. New York: Dover.

Plato. 1920. "Parmenides." In *The Dialogues of Plato*, vol. 2, 85–140. Translated by B. Jowett. New York: Random House.

————. 1974. *Republic*. Translated by G. M. A. Grube. Indianapolis: Hackett.

————. 1990. *The Theaetetus of Plato*. Translated by M. J. Levett. Indianapolis: Hackett.

————. 1993. *Sophist*. Translated by Nicholas P. White. Indianapolis: Hackett.

Robinson, Zack, Corey J. Maley, and Gualtiero Piccinini. 2015. "Is Consciousness A Spandrel?" *Journal of the American Philosophical Association* 1, no. 2 (Summer): 365–83.

Rubercy, Eryck de, and Dominique Le Buhan. 1983. *Douze Questions Posée à Jean Beaufret à propos de Martin Heidegger*. Paris: Editions Aubier.

Sartre, Jean-Paul. 1956. *Being and Nothingness: An Essay on Phenomenological Ontology*. Translated by Hazel Barnes. New York: Philosophical Library.

Searle, John. 1979. *Expression and Meaning*. New York: Cambridge University Press.

————. 1995. "The Mystery of Consciousness: Part II." *The New York Review of Books*, November 16. http://www.nybooks.com/articles/1995/11/16/the-mystery-of-consciousness-part-ii/.

Sheehan, Thomas. 2015. *Making Sense of Heidegger: A Paradigm Shift*. New York: Rowman & Littlefield.

Spinoza, Baruch. 1982. *The Ethics and Selected Letters*. Translated by Samuel Shirley. Edited by Seymour Feldman. Indianapolis: Hackett.

Sullivan, Shannon, and Nancy Tuana, eds. 2007. *Race and Epistemologies of Ignorance*. Albany: State University of New York Press.

Thayer, H. S., ed. 1970. *Pragmatism: The Classic Writings*. New York: New American Library.

Thompson, Evan, Antoine Lutz, and Diego Cosmelli. 2005. "Neurophenomenology: An Introduction for Neurophilosophers." In *Cognition and the Brain: The Philosophy and Neuroscience Movement*, edited by Andres Brook and Kathleen Akins, 40–97. New York: Cambridge University Press.

Varela, F. J. 1996. "Neurophenomenology: A Methodological Remedy to the Hard Problem." *Journal of Consciousness Studies* 3: 330–50.

Velmans, Max. 2009. *Understanding Consciousness*. New York: Routledge.

Waal, Frans de. 2016. *Are We Smart Enough to Know How Smart Animals Are*? New York: Norton.

Wittgenstein, Ludwig. 2009. *Philosophical Investigations*. Translated by G. E. M. Anscombe, P. M. S. Hacker, and Joachim Schulte. Oxford: Wiley-Blackwell.

Index

NANCY J. HOLLAND is Professor Emerita of Philosophy at Hamline University. Her most recent books are *Ontological Humility: Lord Voldemort and the Philosophers* and *The Madwoman's Reason: The Concept of the Appropriate in Ethical Thought.*

Lightning Source UK Ltd.
Milton Keynes UK
UKHW04f0847310718
326548UK00001B/65/P